THE BOOK OF
NAVY SONGS

COLLECTED AND EDITED BY
THE TRIDENT SOCIETY
OF THE UNITED STATES NAVAL ACADEMY
AT ANNAPOLIS, MARYLAND
NAVAL INSTITUTE PRESS

INTRODUCTION

THE BOOK OF NAVY SONGS is a collection of the most typical and popular songs sung by the officers and men of the United States Navy. It is a musical history of our Navy from its birth down to the present day. Not only are these the songs sung in the wardroom and on liberty, but they are the songs sung wherever Navy men have served: on frigate and dreadnaught; in fo'c's'le and camp; on the seven seas or with the Army in Tripoli, China, and France. Here the poles meet with the tropics, and East meets with the West. The men of John Paul Jones sail with Dewey at Manila Bay, and the ghosts of early frigates join column with the carriers of Midway and the Philippine Sea. And because the men of the Navy and the men of the Merchant Service have been inseparably commingled since America's first days at sea, the shanties of the fast flying clippers find rightful place here alongside the songs of the warship. It is a cosmopolitan collection, because the songs the Navy sings are as varied as the work of the Navy itself, and as the men who perform its many duties.

This revision to THE BOOK OF NAVY SONGS is more than just a musical history of the Navy, however. It is also a musical "Bible" for the midshipmen at the Naval Academy; the entire first section of the book is devoted to their music. Their "fight" songs and some of the music of their chief rivals—the West Point "Kaydets"—are here, as well as the music of the Navy's sister services and a few songs which, though not football songs, are sung by the inhabitants of "Crabtown-on-the-Bay."

The second part of the book, "Wardroom Songs," is arranged chronologically, from the shanties of the sailing days to the songs of the post-World War II period. An attempt has been made to include in this section only those songs which are currently popular—those which might be heard wherever a few Navy men should be gathered about a piano or "uke." The piano arrangements are purposely simple to enable as many people as possible to use and enjoy this music, and the chord letters have been added to help those who play other instruments. The chord chart in the back of the book is a supplement to this aid. In using the book, don't hesitate to try songs whose names are unfamiliar. You may find that the melody is quite familiar, but that you know different lyrics. And you will probably find that even if the tune is unfamiliar, you will like the song. There is a wealth of wonderful music here.

The existence of this new edition was made possible only by the encouragement and interest of VAdm. Charles Turner Joy, Superintendent of the Naval Academy, and RAdm. Charles A. Buchanan, Commandant of Midshipmen. LCol. James B. Glennon, USMC, Officer Representative of the Trident Society when the idea for this revision was born in the spring of 1953, helped give it a good start with his enthusiastic support. Cdr. Franklin F. Penney, the succeeding Officer Representative, had a no less enthusiastic interest in the book, and rendered invaluable assistance in its production throughout the following year. To Mr. Joseph W. Crosley we are also greatly indebted: it was he who arranged and harmonized the music for the original editions, upon which, naturally, this revision is built. Others whose assistance deserve attention are: Mid'n Wesley A. Newsome, President of the Trident Society; Midshipmen Tom J. Lapham, Donald M. Lynne, and James K. McPherson, who did all the art work for the revision; Mid'n Robert E. Mack; Mid'n D. L. Fahrney; the Naval Institute staff (especially Cdr. Roy deS. Horn and Cdr. Joseph K. Taussig, Jr.); LCdr. A. C. Morris, Luke L. Lockwood, MUC, and Everett McLaughlin, MU1, of the Naval Academy band; Assistant Professor Donald C. Gilley, the Naval Academy Choirmaster; Capt. and Mrs. W. H. McClain; Lt. and Mrs. L. W. Zech; and Mrs. C. F. Turk. Finally, the Trident Society is indebted to the authors and publishers of the copyrighted material used in this book for their friendly cooperation and for their generosity in allowing their material to be used in this collection.

KLEBER S. MASTERSON, JR.
Midshipman, USN
Vice President, Trident Society
Editor, 1955 Revision

3 May 1954

CONTENTS

NAVAL ACADEMY SONGS

The Star Spangled Banner

By
Francis Scott Key

On the shore dimly seen through the mists of the deep,
    Where the foe's haughty host in dread silence reposes,
What is that which the breeze, o'er the towering steep,
    As it fitfully blows, half conceals, half discloses?
Now it catches the gleam of the morning's first beam,
    In full glory reflected, now shines on the stream;
And the Star Spangled Banner, Oh, long may it wave,
    O'er the land of the free, and the home of the brave!

And where is that band who so vauntingly swore,
    That the havoc of war and the battle's confusion,
A home and a country shall leave us no more?
    Their blood has wash'd out their foul foot-step's pollution!
No refuge could save the hireling and slave,
    From the terror of flight, or the gloom of the grave;
And the Star Spangled Banner, in triumph doth wave,
    O'er the land of the free, and the home of the brave!

O thus be it e'er, when freemen shall stand,
    Between their lov'd home, and the war's desolation;
Blest with vict'ry and peace, may the Heav'n rescued land,
    Praise the pow'r that hath made, and preserved us a Nation;
Then conquer we must, for our cause it is just,
    And this be our motto:- In God is our trust;
And the Star Spangled Banner, in triumph shall wave,
    O'er the land of the free, and the home of the brave!

The National Anthem is naturally the piece of music oftenest heard in the Navy, played as it is at "Colors" and at the conclusion of every official entertainment. The origin of the song needs no explanation here.

Anchor's Aweigh

words by
Capt. ALFRED H. MILES, USN(Ret)

Music by
CHAS. A. ZIMMERMAN

Anchor's Aweigh

Get under way, Navy,
   Decks cleared for the fray,
We'll hoist true Navy Blue
   So Army down your Grey-y-y-y.
Full speed ahead, Navy;
   Army heave to,
Furl Black and Grey and Gold
   And hoist the Navy, hoist the Navy Blue.

Blue of the Seven Seas,
   Gold of God's great sun —
Let these our colors be
   Till all of time be done-n-n-ne,
By Severn shore we learn
   Navy's stern call:
Faith, courage, service true
   With honor over, honor over all.

"Anchor's Aweigh" is entirely a Naval Academy production, and as first written in 1907 was intended as the 1907 Class march. The tune was composed by Lieut. Zimmerman, Bandmaster of the Naval Academy Band and Choir Director, who composed a march each year for the graduating class. Captain A. H. Miles, then a midshipman, wrote the words with the exception of the last verse which was written by Midshipman R. Lovell, class of 1926.

Navy Blue And Gold

Words by
Cdr. Roy DeS. Horn, USN(Ret)

Music by
J. W. Crosley

So hoist our colors, hoist them high,
   And vow allegiance true,
So long as sunset gilds the sky
   Above the ocean blue,
Unlowered shall those colors be
   Whatever fate they meet,
So glorious in victory,
   Triumphant in defeat.

Four years together by the Bay
   Where Severn joins the tide,
Then by the Service called away,
   We've scattered far and wide;
But still when two or three shall meet,
   And old tales be retold,
From low to highest in the Fleet
   Will pledge the Blue and Gold.

Up And At 'Em, Navee!

Words by
W. G. Beecher, Jr., '25

Music by
P. B. KLAKRING, '27

A Cheer For Navy

A cheer, a cheer for Navy   Sing her praise on high. Shout o'er the sev-en seas, For Na-vy we will do and die. So clear the decks for ac-tion   All our foes will be   Sunk be-neath our roar-ing guns While Na-vy's sail-ing on to vic-to-ry.

A cheer, a cheer, for Navy;
  Sailing on to score
Our course is dead ahead
  And we will head for victory's shore.
So rip the line asunder
  Soon their team will be
Flound'ring while our guns will thunder
  For another Navy victory.

Navy Victory March

Words by Lt. W. R. SIMA, U.S.N. and
Midshipmen COLLINS and MARTIN, U.S.N.

Music by
Lt. W. R. SIMA, U.S.N.

Eyes of the Fleet

Words and Music by
RAdm. J. V. McELDUFF

hearts ev - er beat for the Eyes Of The Fleet,

Eyes Of The Fleet o-ver the na - vy. vy.

Fight, fight, fight, fight for the navy,
   Big team in navy gold and blue,
Fight, fight, fight, fight for the navy,
   The fleet depends on you.
Fight, fight, fight, fight for the navy,
   We know that you'll come through,
The pride of the fleet, you're a team that can't be beat,
   On to victory, fight for the navy.

   The first version of this song refers to the Navy's young air arm in the period prior to World War II. At that time, before radar was in general use, the Navy's scout planes were truly its "eyes."

Song Of The Navy

Words by
HAVEN GILLESPIE

Music by
BYRON GAY

Blacksmith Song

Salvo Song
(Don't Give Up The Ship)

Words by
AL DUBIN

Music by
HARRY WARREN

Lyrics (as sung in the music):
Ship-mates stand to-geth-er, Don't give up the ship. Fair or storm-y weath-er We won't give up, we won't give up the ship; Friends and pals for-ev-er, It's a long, long trip. If you have to take a lick-in' Car-ry on and quit your kickin' Don't give up the ship.

Navy Version.
Words by Commander O. C. Badger, U.S.N.

FIRE those Navy salvos;
CRASH! they rip and roar!
BOOM! those Navy broadsides
Must tear apart the Army team and score
Fight on for the Navy,
Fighters all are we;
SOCK the Army! BLOCK the Army!
ROCK the Army! And we'll carry
On to victory!

Gangway Song

Words by
R. E. Mack and W. G. Beecher, Jr., '25

Music by
W. R. SIMA

19

Blue and Gold Fight Song

Words by
R. E. MACK

Music by
R. B. LEWIS

This song (with slightly different words) was introduced in the Musical Club Show of 1954. Midshipman R. E. Mack wrote this version in response to the Brigade's desire for more songs adaptable to contests with schools other than Army.

Army Mule

Naturally many of the Naval Academy "fight" songs are directed toward the most important of Navy's football games—the Army-Navy Game. This song, and the two that follow it, illustrate the midshipmen's attitude toward the West Point mascot, the Army mule, and toward their own mascot, Bill the Goat.

The Goat Is Old And Gnarly

The Old Gray Mare

The applicability of this old favorite to the friendly rivalry with the "Kaydets" is obvious.

There's An Aggregation

There's an ag - gre - ga - tion known through - out the
coun - try, Al - ways read - y for a fro - lic or a fray, From their
high and might - y sta - tion they are known through - out the na - tion As the
boys from down in Crab - town - on - the - Bay. Each year they sal - ly forth to face the
Ar - my And turn the Ar - my mule in - to a lamb, In the
midst of scrap and scrim - mage You will see the bus - y im - age, Of the

"Crabtown-on-the-Bay" is Annapolis, the site of the U. S. Naval Academy. It is on Chesapeake Bay. The "spoiled and pampered pets of Uncle Sam" phrase has been a tradition at the Naval Academy ever since an irate congressman first used it in a scathing denunciation of the Midshipmen. The Military Academy cadets are referred to as the "Army" and as the "Grey-legs." The latter nickname refers to the grey uniforms worn by the cadets.

We Are The Old Nyvee

We Are From Crabtown

Up With The Navy
(Up With Montana)

Music by
DICK HOWELL

day And the bray of the mule Will be heard from the field when the

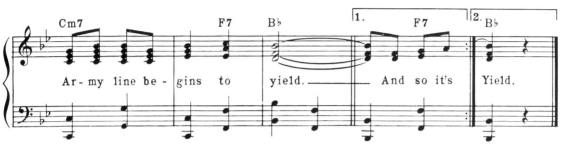

Ar- my line be - gins to yield._____ And so it's Yield.

The Pride Of The Navy

The poor Army mule, he will never say die,
    But look out for the goat with the blood in his eye,
He's noted for grit and he'll fight to the end,
    Whoa mule! step aside or he'll get you again!

The Army knows all about war on the land,
    But sea-going tactics they can't understand,
So into it, Navy, and do them up right,
    We're up here to lick them, so fight, Navy, fight!

Dukke Lisse

Music by
ELITH WORSING

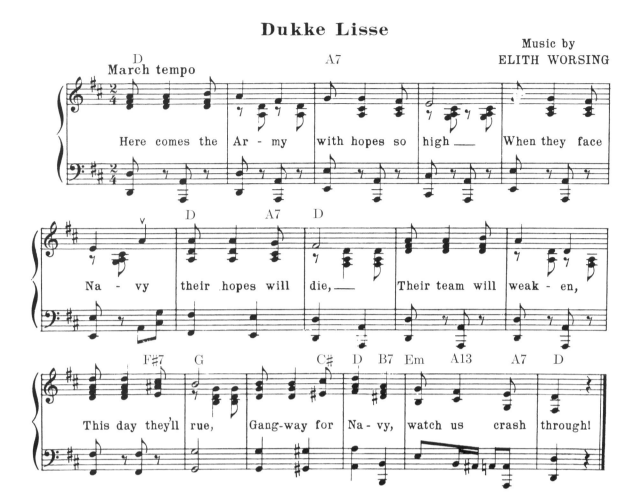

Here comes the Ar-my with hopes so high___ When they face Na-vy their hopes will die,___ Their team will weak-en, This day they'll rue, Gang-way for Na-vy, watch us crash through!

Here comes the Navy set for a scrap,
We're feeling fit to wipe up the map;
Kaydets, we'll prove that Army's a dud!
Gangway for Navy, we're out for blood!

The Service Boast

Words by
A. K. Morehouse, '22

ships at Tim-buc-too, And we'll drink a mer-ry toast to our team, the Ser-vice boast, And the wear-ers of the good old Na-vy Blue.

The annual football game between the United States Naval and Military Academies is one of the great features of the year, and the results are quickly cabled all over the world to wherever the graduates may be serving. All of our ships stationed both in the Philippines and China are said to be on the "China Station." "Crabtown" is the midshipmen's name for Annapolis.

Touchdown Song

Music by
D. WILKERSON, '20.

West Point Alma Mater

Words by
PAUL S. REINECKE

Music by
FERD. KÜCKEN
Arr. by F. C. MAYER

2. Guide us, thy sons a-right,
Teach us by day, by night,
To keep thine honor bright,
For thee to fight.
When we depart from thee,
Serving on land or sea,
May we still loyal be,
West Point, to thee!

This song of the United States Military Academy at West Point and the songs that follow are included out of compliment to our brothers-in-arms and because midshipmen and Naval Academy graduates have heard them sung so often by the serried gray on the opposite side of many a football field.

Arrangement used by permission of F. C. Mayer and Capt. Philip Egner.

Army Blue

Arr. by
PHILIP EGNER

We've not much long-er here to stay, For in a month or two, We'll
bid fare-well to "Ca-det Gray," And don the Ar-my Blue.

CHORUS

Ar - my Blue, Ar - my Blue, Hur-rah for the Ar-my Blue; We'll
bid fare-well to "Ca-det Gray," And don the "Ar - my Blue."

Army Blue

With pipe and song we'll jog along
    Till this short time is thru',
And all among our jovial throng
    Have donned the Army Blue.

To Ethics, Mineralogy,
    And Engineering, too,
We'll bid good-bye without a sigh,
    And don the Army Blue.

To the ladies who come up in June
    We'll bid a fond adieu,
And hoping they'll be married soon,
    And join the Army too.

Here's to the man who wins the cup,
    May he be kind and true,
And may he bring "Our God-son" up
    To don the Army Blue.

Now, fellows, we must say good-bye,
    We've stuck our four years thru',
Our future is a cloudless sky,
    We'll don the Army Blue.

'Twas the song we sang in old plebe camp,
    When first our gray was new,
The song we sang on summer nights,
    That song of Army Blue.

O'er camp and highland watched the stars
    That watched our far homes too,
And lonely voices joined full bold
    In singing "Army Blue."

Those summer days have long gone by,
    And years have vanished too,
Oh, long ago we doffed the gray
    And donned the Army Blue.

But still I hear that olden song,
    I feel the evening dew,
And mellow strings and voices join
    Again in "Army Blue."

Benny Havens, Oh!

Adapted from the tune of
"The Wearing of the Green"
Arr. by F.C. Mayer

Come fill your glass-es, fel-lows, and stand up in a
In the Ar-my there's so-bri-e-ty, pro-mo-tion's ver-y

row, To — sing-ing sen-ti-men-tal-ly we're go-ing for to go.
slow, So we'll sing our rem-i-nis-cenc-es of Ben-ny Ha-vens, Oh!

CHORUS

Oh! Ben-ny Ha-vens, Oh!— Oh! Ben-ny Ha-vens, Oh! We'll

sing our rem-i-nis-cenc-es of Ben-ny Ha-vens, Oh!

Let us toast our foster father, the Republic, as you know,
  Who in the paths of science taught us upward for to go;
And the maidens of our native land, whose cheeks like roses glow,
  They're oft remembered in our cups at Benny Havens, Oh!

To the ladies of our Army our cups shall ever flow,
  Companions in our exile and our shield 'gainst every woe;
May they see their husbands generals, with double pay also,
  And join us in our choruses at Benny Havens, Oh!

Come fill up to our Generals, God bless the brave heroes,
  They're an honor to their country, and a terror to their foes;
May they long rest on their laurels, and troubles never know,
  But live to see a thousand years at Benny Havens, Oh!

To our kind old Alma Mater, our rock-bound Highland home,
  We'll cast back many a fond regret as o'er life's sea we roam;
Until on our last battle-field the lights of heaven shall glow,
  We'll never fail to drink to her and Benny Havens, Oh!

Benny Havens, Oh!

May the Army be augmented, promotion be less slow,
   May our country in the hour of need be ready for the foe;
May we find a soldier's resting-place beneath a soldier's blow,
   With room enough beside our graves for Benny Havens, Oh!

And if amid the battle shock our honor e'er should trail,
   And hearts that beat beneath its folds should turn or basely quail;
Then may some son of Benny's, with quick avenging blow,
   Lift up the flag we loved so well at Benny Havens, Oh!

To our comrades who have fallen, one cup before we go,
   They poured their life-blood freely out pro bono publico;
No marble points the stranger to where they rest below,
   They lie neglected far away from Benny Havens, Oh!

When you and I and Benny, and all the others too,
   Are called before the "final board" our course in life to view,
May we never "fess" on any point, but straight be told to go,
   And join the army of the blest at Benny Havens, Oh!

This song, like "Army Blue," we are printing here because it is dear to our friends and rivals, the Cadets of the United States Military Academy. In addition it is beloved by every alumnus of West Point; and there are few midshipmen or naval officers who have not become acquainted with it. Benny Havens, it is understood, was originally a sutler on the West Point reservation and very popular with the cadets of earlier days; but in the course of hallowing years the name has in a way become synonymous with West Point itself.

Slum and Gravy

Words by
HAMILTON S. HAWKINS, Jr.
FRANCIS E. HOWARD
MEREDITH D. MASTERS

Adapted from the
"Song of the Vagabonds"
by RUDOLPH FRIML
and BRIAN HOOKER

The Marine's Hymn

Our flag's unfurl'd to ev'ry breeze,
From dawn to setting sun,
We have fought in ev'ry clime and place
Where we could take a gun;
In the snow of far off northern lands,
And in sunny tropic scenes,
You will find us always on the job—
The United States Marines.

The Marine's Hymn

Here's health to you and to our corps,
  Which we are proud to serve;
In many a strife we've fought for life,
  And never lost our nerve.
If the Army and the Navy
  Ever look on Heaven's scenes,
They will find the streets are guarded
  By United States Marines.

The first two lines of the song refer to the participation of United States Marines in the War with Mexico and the War with the Barbary Pirates.

This is the song of the Marine Corps. Col. Henry C. Davis, U. S. Marine Corps, writes as follows:

"The Marine's Hymn is, of course, a more or less famous song historically. I have never been able to trace the origin of the song beyond the words of the first two lines, 'From the Halls of Montezuma to the Shores of Tripoli', which was inscribed on the corps colors from a date of many years ago. The following verse I wrote at Camp Meyer in 1911 when on an expedition."

Courtesy of the United States Marine Corps.

The U.S. Air Force

Words and Music by
ROBERT CRAWFORD
Arr. by MAXWELL ECKSTEIN

The Caissons Go Rolling Along

Words and Music by
EDMUND L. GRUBER

1. Ov-er hill, ov-er dale, we have hit the dust-y trail, And those
2. To the front, day and night, where the dough-boys dig and fight, And those

Cais-sons go roll-ing a - long. "Coun-ter March! Right a-bout!" Hear those
Cais-sons go roll-ing a - long. Our bar-rage will be there fired

wag-on sol-diers shout, While those Cais-sons go roll-ing a - long. For it's
on the rock-et's flare, Where those Cais-sons go roll-ing a - long.

CHORUS

Hi! Hi! Hee! In the Field Ar-til-ler - y, Call off your num-bers loud and

strong! And where-e'er we go You will al-ways know That those Caissons are

roll-ing a - long; That those Cais-sons are roll-ing a - long.

Semper Paratus

Words and Music by
Capt. E.S. Van BOSKERCK, U.S.C.G.
Arr. by J. ROCHETTE

From Aztec shore to Arctic Zone, To Europe and Far East, The Flag is carried by our ships In times of war and peace: And never have we struck it yet In spite of foemen's might. Who cheered our crews and cheered again For showing how to fight. So here's the Coast Guard marching song. We

Gentlemen Sailors

Allegro moderato

We have | Stud-ied Na-vi-ga-tion, Sea-man— | ship and col-lege math, | ___

Eng-lish, Span-ish, French and Na-val Law; We have | learned to in-te-grate and to

dif-fer-en- ti-ate, And of | ord-nance we no long-er are in | awe. But in

spite of all we know, on the | cruis-es we must go, And we'll

have to learn a-bout life on the | foam. We shall | al-so get to see, in a

far-a-way coun-try, That | we can sure have fun a-way from | home! **We're**

We can navigate a ship from the time it leaves its slip,
   'Til it's back again as safe as can be,
Steer a straight course through a fog with a sextant, lead and log,
   And are never known to miss our fix at sea.
We can name for you each star, and can tell you just how far
   Each planet is from us and from the sun;
We can take an azimuth, scarcely ever have to bluff—
   Navigation's of them all the simplest one.

Old Cruise Song

A song reminiscent of the summer practice cruises taken annually by the midshipmen. These cruises, in time of peace, go either to Europe or to South America and are an important part of the training program for the future officers. Naturally the cruises are full of happy times, but even so the midshipmen look forward to their end because the annual leave begins then. Bancroft Hall is the huge dormitory of the Naval Academy.

The Life Boat's Crew

And we're ready one and all,
  When we hear the bo's'n's call;
For we're members of the life boat's crew.

Yes, we're ready every man,
  To save you if we can,
For we're members of the life boat's crew.

This song can be heard in the mess-hall when the Brigade is dining. It is a humorous part of the "man-overboard drill," which the plebes learn as part of their training.

No More Rivers

No More Rivers

Almost out of the wilderness,
   Out of the wilderness, Out of the wilderness,
Almost out of the wilderness,
   Five more rivers to cross,
Five more rivers, there's five more rivers to cross,
   Five more rivers, there's five more rivers to cross.

Thank God, we're out of the wilderness,
   Out of the wilderness, Out of the wilderness,
Thank God, we're out of the wilderness,
   No more rivers to cross,
No more rivers, no more rivers to cross,
   No more rivers, no more rivers to cross.

This is a favorite with the midshipmen because it means that Graduation is near. It is sung by the first class (or by the plebes for the first class) as they take their last two sets of term examinations. As each examination is finished, they drop one from the number of rivers until there are "no more rivers to cross." Alumni will see that this is a change from the tradition when they were midshipmen: previously a "river" was an entire group of term examinations, and no one could sing the song until he had finished his first year (when he had "six more rivers to cross").

For Those In Peril On The Sea

Academy Hymn

Eternal Father, strong to save, Whose arm hath bound the restless wave,
Who bidd'st the mighty ocean deep Its own appointed limits keep;
Oh, hear us when we cry to Thee, For those in peril on the sea, A-men.

O Christ! Whose voice the waters heard
  And hushed their raging at Thy word,
Who walked'st on the foaming deep,
  And calm amidst its rage didst sleep;
Oh, hear us when we cry to Thee
  For those in peril on the sea!

Most Holy Spirit! Who didst brood
  Upon the chaos dark and rude,
And bid its angry tumult cease,
  And give, for wild confusion, peace;
Oh, hear us when we cry to Thee
  For those in peril on the sea!

O Trinity of love and power!
  Our brethren shield in danger's hour;
From rock and tempest, fire and foe,
  Protect them wheresoe'er they go;
Thus evermore shall rise to Thee
  Glad hymns of praise from land and sea.

This hymn is an appropriate one with which to end the section of Naval Academy Songs. It was written in 1860 by the Reverend William Whiting, clergyman of the Church of England, after he had come through a terrible storm in the Mediterranean Sea. Every service at the Naval Academy is closed with the first stanza of the hymn, the entire congregation kneeling or seated with bowed heads. From the Academy the custom has spread to many ships of the Fleet.

WARDROOM SONGS

Sailing

The sailor's life is bold and free,
    His home is on the rolling sea;
And never heart more true or brave
    Than his who launches on the wave;
Afar he speeds in distant climes to roam,
    With jocund song he rides the sparkling foam.

The tide is flowing with the gale,
    Y'heave ho! my lads, set ev'ry sail;
The harbor bar we soon shall clear;
    Farewell, once more, to home so dear,
For when the tempest rages loud and long,
    That home shall be our guiding star and song.

One of the oldest and most favored of sea-songs, both inside the Service and outside.

Blow The Man Down

I'm a deep water sailor just come from Hong-Kong —
To me way-aye, blow the man down!
If you'll give me some whiskey, I'll sing you a song —
Oh! give me some time to blow the man down!

'Twas on board a Black Baller I first served my time —
To me way-aye, blow the man down!
And in the Black Baller I wasted my prime —
Oh! give me some time to blow the man down!

'Tis when a Black Baller's preparing for sea —
To me way-aye, blow the man down!
You'd split your sides laughing the sights you would see —
Oh! give me some time to blow the man down!

With the tinkers and tailors and soldiers, and all —
To me way-aye, blow the man down!
That ship for good seamen aboard a Black Ball —
Oh! give me some time to blow the man down!

'Tis when a Black Baller is clear of the land —
To me way-aye, blow the man down!
The crew musters aft at the word of command —
Oh! give me some time to blow the man down!

"Lay aft!" is the cry, "to the break of the poop!" —
To me way-aye, blow the man down!
"Or I'll help you along with the toe of my boot!" —
Oh! give me some time to blow the man down!

"Pay attention to orders now, you, one and all" —
To me way-aye, blow the man down!
"For see right above you there flies the Black Ball" —
Oh! give me some time to blow the man down!

Blow The Man Down

'Tis larboard and starboard on the deck you will sprawl __
    To me way-aye, blow the man down!
For Kicking Jack Williams commands the Black Ball __
    Oh! give me some time to blow the man down!

Aye, first it's a fist and then it's a fall __
    To me way-aye, blow the man down!
When you ship as a sailor aboard the Black Ball __
    Oh! give me some time to blow the man down!

(Second Version)
As I was a-walking down Paradise Street __
    To me way-aye, blow the man down!
A pretty young damsel I chanced for to meet __
    Oh! give me some time to blow the man down!

She was round in the counter and bluff in the bow__
    To me way-aye, blow the man down!
So I took in all sail and cried "Way enough now"__
    Oh! give me some time to blow the man down!

I hailed her in English, she answered me clear __
    To me way-aye, blow the man down!
"I'm from the Black Arrow bound to Shakespeare"__
    Oh! give me some time to blow the man down!

So I tailed her my flipper and took her in tow __
    To me way-aye, blow the man down!
And yardarm to yardarm away we did go__
    Oh! give me some time to blow the man down!

But as we were going she said unto me __
    To me way-aye, blow the man down!
"There's a spanking full-rigger just ready for sea"__
    Oh! give me some time to blow the man down!

That spanking full-rigger to New York was bound __
    To me way-aye, blow the man down!
She was very well manned and very well found __
    Oh! give me some time to blow the man down!

But as soon as that packet was clear of the bar __
    To me way-aye, blow the man down!
The mate knocked me down with the end of a spar __
    Oh! give me some time to blow the man down!

As soon as that packet was out on the sea__
    To me way-aye, blow the man down!
'Twas devilish hard treatment of every degree __
    Oh! give me some time to blow the man down!

So I give you fair warning before we belay__
    To me way-aye, blow the man down!
Don't never take heed of what pretty girls say __
    Oh! give me some time to blow the man down!

One of the oldest and most popular of the shanties. "Blow" means to "strike" or "knock." The Black Ball Line was a famous line of packets between New York and Liverpool. The second version relates the sad experience of a too-trusting sailor who was persuaded by a pretty girl to ship on a clipper which later proved to be a "hell-ship."

Blow, Boys, Blow

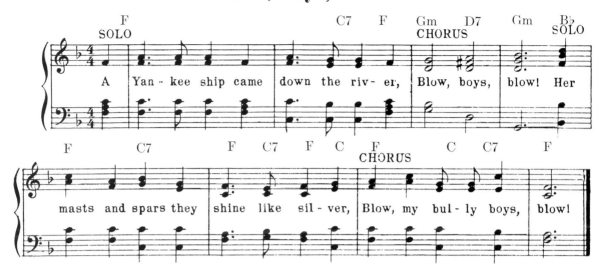

How do you know she's a Yankee liner?
  Blow, boys, blow!
The Stars and Stripes float out behind her.
  Blow, my bully boys, blow!

And who d'you think is the captain of her?
  Blow, boys, blow!
Why, Bully Hayes is the captain of her.
  Blow, my bully boys, blow!

And who d'you think is the mate aboard her?
  Blow, boys, blow!
Santander James is the mate aboard her.
  Blow, my bully boys, blow!

Santander James, he's a rocket from hell, sir,
  Blow, boys, blow!
He'll ride you down as you ride the spanker.
  Blow, my bully boys, blow!

And what d'you think they've got for dinner?
  Blow, boys, blow!
Pickled eels' feet and bullock's liver.
  Blow, my bully boys, blow!

Then blow my bullies, all together,
  Blow, boys, blow!
And blow for all tars in sorrow.
  Blow, my bully boys, blow!

All Hands On Deck

All hands on deck,
  There's a pretty little girl in sight.
All hands on deck,
  For she certainly looks all right.
What do we care
  If the ship becomes a wreck,
For I haven't seen a girl in the last six months.
  All hands on deck!

A Capital Ship

A cap-i-tal ship for an o-cean trip, Was the *Wal-lop-ing Win-dow Blind!* No — wind that blew dis-mayed the crew, Or — trou-bled the — cap-tain's mind; The — man at the wheel was made to feel Con-tempt for the wild-est — blow-ow-ow, Tho' it of-ten ap-peared, when the gale had cleared, That he'd been in his bunk be-low.

CHORUS

Then blow, ye winds, heigh-ho! A-rov-ing I will go! I'll stay no more on Eng-land's shore, So let the mu-sic play-ay-ay! I'm

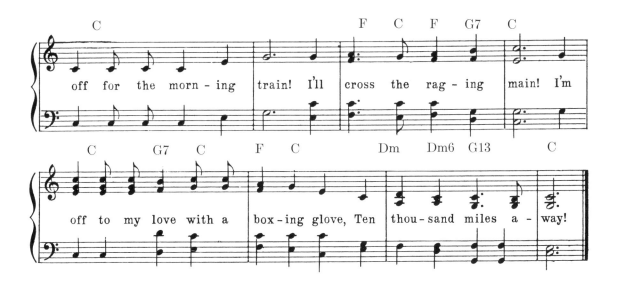

off for the morn-ing train! I'll cross the rag-ing main! I'm off to my love with a box-ing glove, Ten thou-sand miles a-way!

The bos'n's mate was very sedate,
  Yet fond of amusement too;
He played hopscotch with the starboard watch,
  While the captain, he tickled the crew!
And the gunner we had was apparently mad,
  For he sat on the after rail,
And fired salutes with the captain's boots,
  In the teeth of the booming gale!

The captain sat on the commodore's hat,
  And dined in a royal way,
Off toasted pigs and pickles and figs
  And gunnery bread each day;
And the cook was Dutch and behaved as such,
  For the diet he gave the crew,
Was a number of tons of hot cross buns
  Served up with sugar and glue.

We all felt ill as mariners will,
  On a diet that's cheap and rude,
And we shivered and shook as we dipped the cook,
  In a tub of his gruesome food;
Then nautical pride we laid aside,
  And we ran the vessel ashore,
On the Gulliby Isles where the Poopoo smiles,
  And the rubbly Ubdugs roar.

Composed of sand was that favored land,
  And trimmed with cinnamon straws,
And pink and blue was the pleasing hue
  Of the tickle-tie-toaster's claws;
And we sat on the edge of a sandy ledge
  And shot at the whistling bee,
And the cinnamon bats wore waterproof hats,
  As they dipped in the bounding sea.

On the Rugby bark from morn till dark,
  We dined till we all had grown
Uncommonly shrunk, when a Chinese junk
  Came up from the Torribly zone;
She was chubby and square, but we didn't much care,
  So we cheerily put out to sea,
And we left all the crew of the junk to chew
  On the bark of the Rugby tree.

Whiskey, Johnny

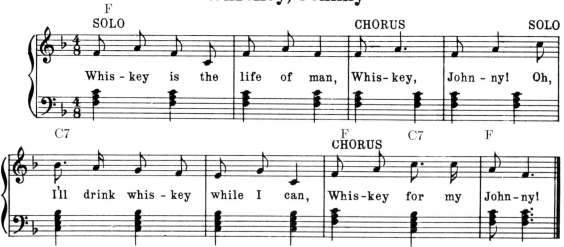

Whiskey from an old tin can,
   Whiskey, Johnny!
I'll drink whiskey when I can,
   Whiskey for my Johnny!

I drink it hot, I drink it cold,
   Whiskey, Johnny!
I drink it new, I drink it old,
   Whiskey for my Johnny!

O whiskey straight and whiskey strong,
   Whiskey, Johnny!
Give me whiskey and I'll sing you a song,
   Whiskey for my Johnny!

Whiskey makes me feel so sad,
   Whiskey, Johnny!
Whiskey killed my poor old dad,
   Whiskey for my Johnny!

Whiskey makes me wear old clothes,
   Whiskey, Johnny!
Whiskey gave me a broken nose,
   Whiskey for my Johnny!

If whiskey comes too near my nose,
   Whiskey, Johnny!
I tip it up and down she goes,
   Whiskey for my Johnny!

I had a girl, her name was Lize,
   Whiskey, Johnny!
She puts whiskey in her pies,
   Whiskey for my Johnny!

My wife and I cannot agree,
   Whiskey, Johnny!
She puts whiskey in her tea,
   Whiskey for my Johnny!

From SONGS OF AMERICAN SAILORMEN, by Joanna C. Colcord, copyright 1938 by
W. W. Norton & Company, Inc. Used by special permission of copyright owners.

Whiskey, Johnny

Here comes the cook with the whiskey can,
  Whiskey, Johnny!
A glass of grog for every man,
  Whiskey for my Johnny!

A glass of grog for every man,
  Whiskey, Johnny!
And a bottle full for the shantyman,
  Whiskey for my Johnny!

A very unusual shanty and long a favorite with sailors when hauling on halliards. The original of this shanty has been traced as far back as the sixteenth century. Apparently the shantyman both approves and condemns his favorite beverage.

A Wet Sheet And A Flowing Sea

A Wet Sheet And A Flowing Sea

Oh, for a soft and gentle wind,
    I heard a fair one cry,
But give to me the roaring breeze,
    And white waves heaving high;
And white waves heaving high, my boys!
    The good ship tight and free;
The world of waters is our home,
    And merry men are we.

There's tempest in yon horned moon,
    And lightning in yon cloud,
And hark the music, mariners,
    The wind is piping loud;
The wind is piping loud, my boys!
    The lightning flashes free,
While the hollow oak our palace is,
    Our heritage the sea.

An old and popular sea-song whose poetic words paint a splendid and vivid picture of ships and the sea and the men who go down in ships to the sea.

The Song Of The Fishes

Come all ye bold fish - er - men, lis - ten to me, ___ While I sing to you a song of the sea; Then blow ye winds west - er - ly, west - er - ly blow, We're bound to the south-'ard, so stead - y we go.

The Song Of The Fishes

First came the bluefish, a-wagging his tail,
  He came up on deck and yells, "All hands make sail!"

Next came the eels with their nimble tails,
  They jumped up aloft and loosed all the sails.

Next came the herrings with their little tails,
  They manned sheets and halliards and set all the sails.

Next came the porpoise, with his short snout,
  He jumped on the bridge and yells, "Ready about."

Next came the swordfish, the scourge of the sea,
  The order that he gave is "hellum's a-lee."

Then came the turbot, as red as a beet,
  He shouted from the bridge, "Stick out that fore-sheet."

And having accomplished these wonderful feats,
  The black bass sang out next to "Rise tacks and sheets."

Next came the whale, the largest of all,
  Singing out from the bridge, "Haul taut mainsail, haul."

Then came the mackerel, with his striped back,
  He flopped on the bridge and yelled, "Board the main tack."

Next came the sprat, the smallest of all,
  He sang out, "Haul well taut, let go and haul."

Then came the cat-fish, with his chuckle-head,
  Out on the main chains for a "heave of the lead."

Next came the flounder, quite fresh from the ground,
  Crying, "Damn your eyes, chuckle-head, mind where you sound!"

Along came the dolphin, flapping his tail,
  He yelled to the boatswain to, "Reef the fore-sail!"

Along came the shark with his three rows of teeth,
  He flopped on the fore-yard and "takes a snug reef."

Up jumped the fisherman, stalwart and grim,
  And with his big net he scooped them all in!

Derelict

Derelict

Fifteen men of a whole ship's list —
    Yo-ho-ho and a bottle of rum!
Dead and be damned and the rest gone whist! —
    Yo-ho-ho and a bottle of rum!
The skipper lay with his nob in gore
Where the scullion's axe his cheek had shore,
And the scullion he was stabbed times four.
    And there they lay and the soggy skies
    Dripped all day long in up-staring eyes,
At murk sunset and at foul sunrise —
    Yo-ho-ho and a bottle of rum!

Fifteen men of 'em stiff and stark —
    Yo-ho-ho and a bottle of rum!
Ten of the crew had the Murder mark —
    Yo-ho-ho and a bottle of rum!
'Twas a cutlass swipe, or an ounce of lead,
Or a yawing hole in a battered head,
And the scuppers glut with a rotting red.
    And there they lay — aye, damn my eyes! —
    All lookouts clapped on paradise,
All souls bound just contrariwise —
    Yo-ho-ho and a bottle of rum!

Fifteen men of 'em good and true —
    Yo-ho-ho and a bottle of rum!
Every man jack could ha' sailed with Old Pew —
    Yo-ho-ho and a bottle of rum!
There was chest on chest of Spanish gold,
With a ton of plate in the middle hold,
And the cabins riot of stuff untold.
    And they lay there that had took the plum,
    With sightless glare and their lips struck dumb,
While we shared all by the rule of thumb —
    Yo-ho-ho and a bottle of rum!

Fifteen men on the dead man's chest —
    Yo-ho-ho and a bottle of rum!
Drink and the devil had done for the rest —
    Yo-ho-ho and a bottle of rum!
We wrapped 'em all in a mains'l tight,
With twice ten turns of a hawser's bight,
And we heaved 'em over and out of sight —
    With a yo-heave-ho! and a fare-you-well!
    And a sullen plunge in the sullen swell,
Ten fathoms deep on the road to hell!
    Yo-ho-ho and a bottle of rum!

This fine old sea ballad was published complete in 1901 as the work of Young E. Allison and Waller, playrights. Allison had received the inspiration from the quatrain of Billy Bones' song in Stevenson's "Treasure Island," but the two departed somewhat from the original subject matter in adding to it. Stevenson credits the original verse to Kingsley's "At Last." The words "Dead Man's Chest," contrary to general belief, refer to an island rendezvous of buccaneers and smugglers in the Caribbean Sea.

The Mermaid

'Twas Fri-day morn when we set sail, And we had not got far from land, When the Cap-tain, he spied a love-ly mer-maid, With a comb and a glass in her hand.

CHORUS

Oh the o-cean waves may roll, And the storm-y winds may blow, While we poor sail-ors go skip-ping up a-loft, And the land lub-bers lay down be-low, be-low, be-low, And the land lub-bers lay down be-low.

The Mermaid

Then up spoke the Captain of our gallant ship,
  And a jolly old Captain was he;
"I have a wife in Salem town,
  But tonight a widow she will be."

Then up spoke the Cook of our gallant ship,
  And a greasy old Cook was he;
"I care more for my kettles and my pots,
  Than I do for the roaring of the sea."

Then up spoke the Cabin-boy of our gallant ship,
  And a dirty little brat was he;
"I have friends in Boston town
  That don't care a ha' penny for me."

Then three times 'round went our gallant ship,
  And three times 'round went she,
And the third time that she went 'round
  She sank to the bottom of the sea.

The swinging chorus to this tune has been familiar throughout the Fleet ever since its adoption at the Naval Academy before World War I.

High Barbaree

"Aloft there, aloft!" our jolly bo's'n cries, —
  Blow high, blow low, and so sailed we;
"Look ahead, look astern, look aweather and alee,
  Keep a lookout down the coast of the High Barbaree!"

"There's naught upon the stern, there's naught upon the lee"—
  Blow high, blow low, and so sailed we;
"But there's a lofty ship to windward, and she's sailing fast and free,
  Cruising down along the coast of the High Barbaree."

"Oh, hail her, oh, hail her," our gallant captain cried —
  Blow high, blow low, and so sailed we;
"Are you a man-o'-war or a privateer," said he,
  "Cruising down along the coast of the High Barbaree?"

"Oh, I am not a man-o'-war, nor privateer," said he —
  Blow high, blow low, and so sailed we;
"I'm a saucy salt sea pirate and looking for my fee,
  Cruising down along the coast of the High Barbaree."

From "Sea Songs and Shanties." Used herein by special permission of the publishers Messrs. Brown, Son & Ferguson, Ltd., 52, Darnley Street, Glasgow, S.1,. Scotland, and not to be reproduced without permission from the publishers.

High Barbaree

"If you are a pirate I'll have you come this way"—
　　Blow high, blow low, and so sailed we;
"Break out your quarter guns, boys, we'll give this pirate play,
　　Cruising down along the coast of the High Barbaree."

Oh, 'twas broadside to broadside, a long time we lay —
　　Blow high, blow low, and so sailed we;
Until the *Prince of Rupert* shot the pirate's mast away,
　　Cruising down along the coast of the High Barbaree.

"Oh, quarter, oh, quarter!" these pirates then did cry —
　　Blow high, blow low, and so sailed we;
But the quarter that we gave them, we sunk them in the sea —
　　Cruising down along the coast of the High Barbaree.

This is more of a ballad than a shanty, and shows its old English origin. The "High Barbaree" was doubtless the coast of the Barbary States of North Africa whose piratical depredations caused one of the first hostile naval expeditions sent out by the United States of America.

Rio Grande

Oh, say, was you ev-er in Ri - o Grande? Way, — you Ri-o! Oh, was you ev - er on — the strand? For we're bound for the Ri-o Grande! And a - way, — you Ri-o! — Way, — you Ri-o! — Sing fare-you-well, my pret-ty young girls, For we're bound for the Ri - o Grande!

From SONGS OF AMERICAN SAILORMEN, by Joanna C. Colcord, copyright 1938 by
W. W. Norton & Company, Inc. Used by special permission copyright owners.

Rio Grande

Oh, New York town is no place for me;
   Way, you Rio!
I'll pack up my bag and go to sea,
   For we're bound for the Rio Grande!

Now, you Bowery ladies, we'll let you know,
   Way, you Rio!
We're bound to the south'ard, O Lord, let her go!
   For we're bound for the Rio Grande!

We'll sell our salt cod for molasses and rum,
   Way, you Rio!
And get home again 'fore Thanksgiving has come,
   For we're bound for the Rio Grande!

Sing good-by to Nellie and good-by to Sue,
   Way, you Rio!
And you who are listening, good-by to you,
   For we're bound for the Rio Grande!

And good-by, fair ladies we know in this town,
   Way, you Rio!
We've left you enough to buy a silk gown,
   For we're bound for the Rio Grande!

Our good ship's a-going out over the bar,
   Way, you Rio!
And we'll point her nose for the south-er-on star,
   For we're bound for the Rio Grande!

Boston

From Bos-ton Har-bour we set sail, When it was blow-ing a dev-il of a gale, With our ring-tail set all a-baft the miz-zen peak, And our Rule Bri-tan-nia plough-ing up the deep. With a big Bow-wow! Tow-row-row! Fal de ral de ri do day!

Up comes the skipper from down below,
    And he looks aloft and he looks alow,
And he looks alow and he looks aloft,
    And it's "Coil up your ropes there, fore-and-aft."

Then down to his cabin he quickly crawls,
    And unto his steward he loudly bawls,
"Go mix me a glass that will make me cough,
    For it's better weather here than it is up aloft."

We poor sailors standing on the deck,
    With the blasted rain all a-pouring down our necks;
Not a drop of grog would he to us afford,
    But he damned our eyes at every other word.

Now the old beggar's dead and gone,
    Darn his eyes, he's left a son,
And if to us he doesn't prove frank,
    We'll very soon make him walk the plank.

And one thing which we have to crave,
    Is that he may have a watery grave,
So we'll heave him down into some dark hole,
    Where the sharks'll have his body and the devil have his soul.

From "Sea Songs and Shanties." Used herein by special permission of the publishers Messrs. Brown, Son & Ferguson, Ltd., 52, Darnley Street, Glasgow, S.1., Scotland, and not to be reproduced without permission from the publishers.

Blow, Ye Winds In The Morning

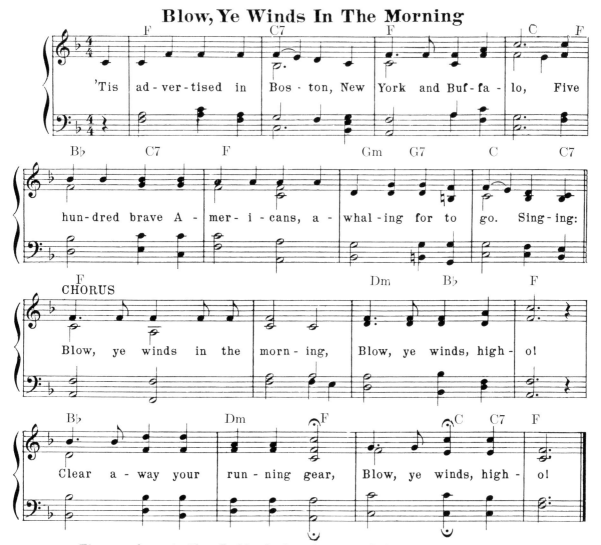

'Tis ad-ver-tised in Bos-ton, New York and Buf-fa-lo, Five
hun-dred brave A-mer-i-cans, a-whal-ing for to go. Sing-ing:

CHORUS

Blow, ye winds in the morn-ing, Blow, ye winds, high-o!
Clear a-way your run-ning gear, Blow, ye winds, high-o!

They send you to New Bedford, that famous whaling port,
And give you to some land-sharks to board and fit you out.

It's now we're out to sea, my boys, the wind comes on to blow;
One half the watch is sick on deck, the other half below.

The Skipper's on the quarterdeck a-squinting at the sails,
When up aloft the lookout sights a school of whales.

"Now clear away the boats, my boys, and after him we'll travel,
But if you get too near his fluke, he'll kick you to the devil!"

Now we have got him turned up, we tow him alongside;
We over with our blubber-hooks and rob him of his hide.

Now the boat steerer overside the tackle overhauls,
The Skipper's in the main-chains, so loudly he does bawl!

Next comes the stowing down, my boys; 'twill take both night and day,
And you'll all have fifty cents apiece on the hundred and ninetieth lay.

But now that our old ship is full and we don't give a damn,
We'll bend on all our stu'nsails and sail for Yankee land.

When we get home, our ship made fast, and we get through our sailing,
A winding glass around we'll pass and damn this blubber whaling!

Poor Old Man

I say, old man, your horse will die, And I say so, and I know so. I say, old man, your horse will die, Oh, poor old man!

And if he dies we'll tan his skin,
And I say so, and I know so.
And if he dies we'll tan his skin,
Oh, poor old man!

And if he lives we'll ride him again!
And I say so, and I know so.
And if he lives we'll ride him again!
Oh, poor old man!

We'll hoist him at the main yardarm,
And I say so, and I know so.
We'll hoist him at the main yardarm,
Oh, poor old man!

And now he's dead we'll bury him deep,
And I say so, and I know so.
And now he's dead we'll bury him deep.
Oh, poor old man!

With this song the sailor celebrated the happy day when he and his shipmates had worked off the advance pay, or "dead horse," advanced by the captain while in port. The "Old Man" was and still is the Captain. The song itself, like most shanties, was never sung on men-o-war.

Samuel Hall

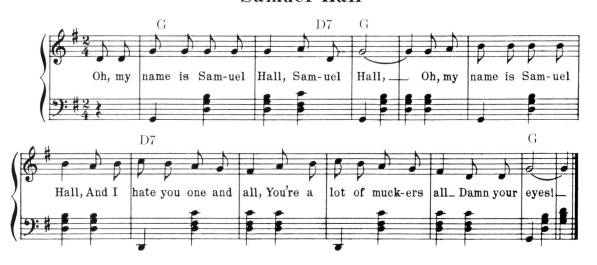

Oh, I killed a man 'tis said, so 'tis said,
  Oh, I killed a man 'tis said, for I hit him on the head,
And I left him there for dead —
  Damn his eyes!

And they put me in the quad, in the **quad**,
  Yes, they put me in the quad with a **chain** and iron **rod**,
And they left me there, by God —
  Damn their eyes!

Oh, the parson he did **come**, he did **come**,
  Oh, the parson he did **come** and he looked so bloody **glum**
As he talked of kingdom come —
  Damn his eyes!

And the Sheriff he came too, he came too,
  And the Sheriff he came too, with his bloody boy in **blue**,
They've a hanging job to do —
  Damn their eyes!

So, it's up the rope I go, up I go,
  So, it's up the rope I go with my friends all down **below**,
Saying, "Sam, I told you so" —
  Damn their eyes!

Oh, let this be my knell, be my knell,
  Oh, let this be my knell, as ye listen to my yell,
Hope to God you **sizzle** well —
  Damn your eyes!

Shenandoah

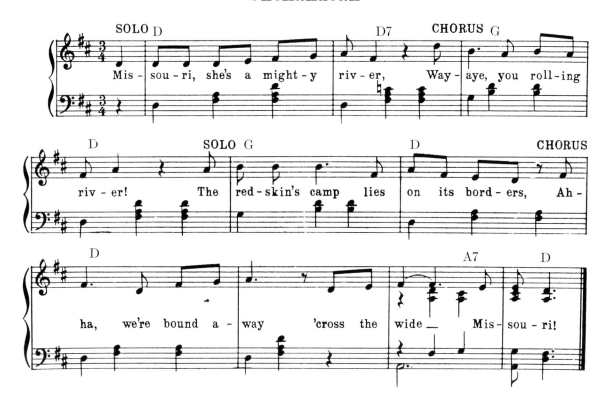

Mis - sou - ri, she's a might - y riv - er, Way - aye, you roll-ing riv - er! The red-skin's camp lies on its bord - ers, Ah - ha, we're bound a - way 'cross the wide __ Mis - sou - ri!

Shenandoah

The white man loved the Indian maid,
   Way-aye, you rolling river!
With notions his canoe was laden.
   Ah-ha, I'm bound away 'cross the wide Missouri!

"Oh, Shenandoah, I love your daughter,"
   Way-aye, you rolling river!
"I'll take her 'cross yon rolling water."
   Ah-ha, I'm bound away 'cross the wide Missouri!

The Chief disdained the trader's dollars,
   Way-aye, you rolling river!
"My daughter you shall never follow."
   Ah-ha, I'm bound away 'cross the wide Missouri!

For seven years I courted Sally,
   Way-aye, you rolling river!
For seven more I longed to have her.
   Ah-ha, I'm bound away 'cross the wide Missouri!

She said she would not be my lover,
   Way-aye, you rolling river!
Because I was a tarry sailor.
   Ah-ha, I'm bound away 'cross the wide Missouri!

A-drinkin' rum and a-chewin' terbaccer,
   Way-aye, you rolling river!
A-drinkin' rum and a-chewin' terbaccer.
   Ah-ha, I'm bound away 'cross the wide Missouri!

At last there came a Yankee skipper,
   Way-aye, you rolling river!
He winked his eye, and he tipped his flipper.
   Ah-ha, I'm bound away 'cross the wide Missouri!

He sold the Chief that fire-water,
   Way-aye, you rolling river!
And 'cross the river he stole his daughter.
   Ah-ha, I'm bound away 'cross the wide Missouri!

Oh, Shenandoah, I long to hear you,
   Way-aye, you rolling river!
Across that wide and rolling river.
   Ah-ha, I'm bound away 'cross the wide Missouri!

One of the most popular of shanties, which probably originated among the early American or Canadian rivermen. Shenandoah apparently was an Indian chief living on the Missouri river, whose daughter was courted first and vainly by a trader. But when a rollicking sea-captain showed up with good liquor instead of money he soon carried away the prize.

Farewell To Grog

Tune-"Come, Landlord
Fill the Flowing Bowl"

Come, mess-mates, pass the bot-tle 'round, Our time is short, re-mem-ber, For our grog must stop, and our spir-its drop, On the first day of Sep-tem-ber.

CHORUS

For to-night we'll mer-ry, mer-ry be, For to-night we'll mer-ry, mer-ry be, For to-night we'll mer-ry, mer-ry be, To-mor-row we'll be sob-er.

Farewell old rye, 'tis a sad, sad word,

But alas! it must be spoken,

The ruby cup must be given up,

And the demijohn be broken.

Jack's happy days will soon be gone,

To return again, oh never!

For they've raised his pay five cents a day,

But stopped his grog forever.

Farewell To Grog

Yet memory oft' will backward turn,
    And dwell with fondness partial,
On the days when gin was not a sin,
    Nor cocktails brought courts-martial.

(Bo's'n-mates pipe "All Hands Splice the Main Brace!")

All hands to splice the main brace, call,
    But splice it now in sorrow,
For the spirit-room key will be laid away
    Forever, on to-morrow.

Grog, a drink of rum and water, was served as a regular ration in the United States Navy until September 1, 1862, when the law abolishing it went into effect. This song was composed and sung in the wardroom of the *U. S. S. Portsmouth* on the night of Aug. 31--- the night before the law took effect. The composer was Caspar Schenk, U.S.N.

The Last Carouse

We meet 'neath the sound-ing raft - er___ And the
But stand by your glass-es stead - y!___ We___

walls___ a - round are bare; As they e - cho our peals of
drink to our com - rades' eyes; Quaff a cup to the dead al -

laugh - ter___ It___ seems that the dead are___ there.
read - y___ And hur - rah for the next that___ dies!

The Last Carouse

Not here are the goblets glowing,
  Not here is the vintage sweet;
'Tis cold as our hearts are growing,
  And dark as the doom we meet.
But stand to your glasses, steady!
  And soon shall our pulses rise;
A cup to the dead already —
  And hurrah! for the next that dies!

There's many a hand that's shaking,
  And many a cheek that's sunk;
But soon, though our hearts are breaking,
  They'll burn with the wine we've drunk.
Then stand to your glasses, steady!
  'Tis here the revival lies;
Quaff a cup to the dead already —
  And hurrah! for the next that dies!

Time was when we laughed at others,
  We thought we were wiser then;
Ha! Ha! let them think of their mothers,
  Who hope to see them again.
No! stand to your glasses, steady!
  The thoughtless is here the wise;
One cup to the dead already —
  And hurrah! for the next that dies!

Not a sigh for the lot that darkles,
  Not a tear for the friends that sink;
We'll fall 'midst the wine cup's sparkles,
  As mute as the wine we drink.
Come, stand to your glasses, steady!
  'Tis this that the respite buys;
A cup to the dead already —
  And hurrah! for the next that dies!

There's a mist on the glass congealing,
  'Tis the hurricane's fiery breath;
And thus does the warmth of feeling,
  Turn ice in the grasp of death.
But stand to your glasses, steady!
  For a moment the vapor flies;
Quaff a cup to the dead already —
  And hurrah! for the next that dies!

Who dreads to the dust returning?
  Who shrinks from the sable shore,
Where the high and haughty yearning
  Of the soul can sting no more?
No, stand to your glasses, steady!
  The world is a world of lies;
A cup to the dead already —
  And hurrah! for the next that dies!

Cut off from the land that bore us,
  Betrayed by the land we find,
Where the brightest have gone before us,
  And the dullest remain behind.
Stand! stand to your glasses, steady!
  'Tis all we have left here to prize;
A cup to the dead already —
  Hurrah! for the next man that dies!

"The Last Carouse" was written years ago at the time when the Plague was raging in India. It bears a certain depressing note due to the tragedies revealed but the magnificent spirit and swing of it make it well worthy of its adoption by the Navy.

My Last Cigar

'Twas off the blue Ca - na - ry Isles, a glo - rious sum - mer day,__ I
sat up - on the quar - ter - deck and whiff'd my cares a - way__ And
as the vol - umed smoke a - rose, like in - cense in the air,__ I
breath'd a sigh to think in sooth, it was my last ci - gar__

CHORUS It was my last ci - gar, it was my last ci - gar__ I
breath'd a sigh to think in sooth, it was my last ci - gar__

My Last Cigar

I lean'd against the quarter rail, and look'd down in the sea,
  E'en there the purple wreath of smoke was curling gracefully;
Oh, what had I at such a time to do with wasting care?
  Alas! the trembling tear proclaim'd it was my last cigar.

I watch'd the ashes, as it came fast drawing t'ward the end,
  I watch'd it as a friend would watch beside a dying friend;
But still the flame crept slowly on, it vanish'd into air,
  I threw it from me—spare the tale—it was my last cigar.

I've seen the land of all I love fade in the distance dim,
  I've watch'd above the blighted heart where once proud hope hath been;
But I've never known a sorrow that could with that compare,
  When off the blue Canary Isles I smoked my last cigar.

This was composed by a naval officer on duty off the coast of Africa before the Civil War, when the United States kept a patrol there to guard against the slave trade. This was very tedious duty, entailing many hardships and long months at sea. Thus the smoking of the composer's last cigar would constitute this a real heart song.

Botany Bay

* (The italicized words are to be *spoken*)

Botany Bay

It's not leaving old England we care about,
  Nor sailing for shores far away,
It's the blooming monotony wears us out,
  And the prospect of Botany Bay.

Oh, the Captain and all the ship's officers,
  The Bo's'n and all of the crew,
The first and second class passengers,
  Knows what us poor convicts go through.

Oh, come all ye dukes and ye duchesses,
  And harken and list to my lay,
Be sure that ye owns all ye touchesses,
  Or they'll land you in Botany Bay.

Oh, had I the wings of a turtle dove,
  Away on my pinions I'd fly,
Straight into the arms of my lady love,
  And there I would languish and die.

Botany Bay was originally a particular British penal settlement near what is now Sydney, Australia, but eventually the name came to mean any Australian convict settlement. The practice of sending convicts to Australia, begun in 1787, was ceased in 1840.

A newer variation on this tune follows:

R. H. I. P.

Oh, the officers ride in a motorboat;
  The Captain, he rides in a gig.
It don't go a doggone bit faster,
  But it makes the old b— feel big!

Oh, the officers ride in a motorboat;
  The Admiral, he rides in his barge.
It don't get there a doggone bit sooner,
  But it makes the old b— feel large!

Oh, the officers eat in the wardroom;
  The Captain, he eats alone.
He don't eat a doggone bit better,
  But he gets to take some of it home!

The enlisted men ride in a motor launch;
  The ensign, he rides in there too.
The ensign, he rides in the sternsheets—
  My gosh! What one stripe will do!

It's not the rolling and pitching we care about,
  Nor the foam on the crest of the waves;
It's the foam in the neck of the bottle,
  That's dragging us down to our graves.

The Midshipmite

The Midshipmite

We launched the cutter an' shoved her out —
  Cheer-i-ly, my lads, yo ho!
The lubbers might ha' heard us shout,
  As the Middy cried, "Now my lads, put about"—
Cheer-i-ly, my lads, yo ho!
  We made for the guns an' we rammed them tight,
But the musket shots came left and right,
  An' down drops the poor little Midshipmite—
Cheer-i-ly, my lads, yo ho!
  Cheer-i-ly, my lads, yo ho!

"I'm done for now; goodbye!"says he —
  Steadily, my lads, yo ho!
"You make for the boat, never mind for me!"
  "We'll take 'ee back, sir, or die!" says we —
Cheer-i-ly, my lads, yo ho!
  So we hoisted him in, in a terrible plight,
An' we pull'd ev'ry man with all his might,
  An' saved the poor little Midshipmite—
Cheer-i-ly, my lads, yo ho!
  Cheer-i-ly, my lads, yo ho!

This is a song that has been "borrowed" from the British Navy. It recounts an incident of the Crimean War when the British Naval Forces were operating against the Russian fortifications.

Sweethearts And Wives

Adapted from Music
by Hubbard P. Smith

Now com-rades, fill your glass - es, And cease each mer - ry jest___ Let
ev - 'ry one a - mong you, Think of her whom he loves best___ From
Maine to Cal - i - for - nia, In lands far off or near,___ God
bless the girls who love us, The girls our hearts hold dear!

CHORUS
Tempo di Valse
Sweet - hearts and wives,___ Where ev - er we may roam,___

Make it a bumper, comrades,
   And each one standing here
Can whisper soft above his glass,
   The name he holds most dear,
While as we drink in silence,
   Across the ocean foam,
Our loving greetings fly tonight,
   We drink to those at home!

Time was when this beautiful drinking song held its regular place in the wardroom mess program. Each Saturday night its solo and melody parts were wafted through the hatch to bring memories and anticipations through thoughts of home to those on deck. It was another of those "ties that bind" in that day of "wooden ships and iron men."

The Maid Of Amsterdam

The Maid Of Amsterdam

Her eyes are like two stars so bright,
   Mark you well what I say!
Her eyes are like two stars so bright,
   Her face is fair, her step is light.

Her cheeks are like the rosebuds' red,
   Mark you well what I say!
Her cheeks are like the rosebuds' red,
   There's wealth of hair upon her head.

I asked this fair maid to take a walk,
   Mark well what I do say!
I asked this fair maid to take a walk,
   That we might have some private talk.

Then I took this fair maid's lily white hand,
   Mark well what I do say!
For I took this fair maid's lily white hand,
   In mine as we walked along the strand.

Then I put my arm around her waist,
   Mark well what I do say!
For I put my arm around her waist,
   And from her lips snatched a kiss in haste.

Then a great big Dutchman rammed my bow,
   Mark well what I do say!
For a great big Dutchman rammed my bow,
   And said, "Young man, dis bin mein vrow!"

Then take a warning, boys, from me,
   Mark well what I do say!
So take a warning, boys, from me,
   With other men's wives don't make too free.

For if you do you will surely rue,
   Mark well what I do say!
For if you do you will surely rue
   Your act, and find my words come true.

Abdul Abulbul Amir

The sons of the Proph-et are brave men and bold, And quite un-ac-
cus-tomed to fear, ____ But the brav-est by far in the
ranks of the Shah, Was Ab-dul A-bul-bul A-mir. ____

If you wanted a man to encourage the van
    Or harass the foe from the rear,
Storm fort or redoubt, you had only to shout
    For Abdul Abulbul Amir.

Now the heroes were plenty and well known to fame
    In the troops that were led by the Czar,
And the bravest of these was a man by the name
    Of Ivan Skavinsky Skavar.

He could jump fifty yards and tell fortunes at cards
    And strum on the Spanish guitar,
In fact quite the cream of this Muscovite team
    Was Ivan Skavinsky Skavar.

One day this bold Russian, he shouldered his gun
    And donned his most truculent sneer,
Downtown he did go where he trod on the toe
    Of Abdul Abulbul Amir.

"Young man," quoth Abdul, "has life grown so dull
    That you wish to end your career?
Vile infidel, know, you have trod on the toe
    Of Abdul Abulbul Amir!"

Abdul Abulbul Amir

"So take your last look at sunshine and brook
　　And send your regrets to the Czar —
For by this I imply, you are going to die,
　　Count Ivan Skavinsky Skavar!"

Then this bold Mameluke drew his trusty skibouk,
　　Singing "Allah! Il Allah! Al-lah!"
And with murderous intent he ferociously went,
　　For Ivan Skavinsky Skavar.

They parried and thrust, they side-stepped and cussed,
　　Of blood they spilled a great part;
The philologist blokes, who seldom crack jokes,
　　Say that hash was first made on that spot.

They fought all that night 'neath the pale yellow moon;
　　The din, it was heard from afar,
And huge multitudes came, so great was the fame,
　　Of Abdul and Ivan Skavar.

As Abdul's long knife was extracting the life,
　　In fact he was shouting "Huzzah!"
He felt himself struck by that wily Calmuck,
　　Count Ivan Skavinsky Skavar.

The Sultan drove by in his red-breasted fly,
　　Expecting the victor to cheer,
But he only drew nigh to hear the last sigh
　　Of Abdul Abulbul Amir.

There's a tomb rises up where the Blue Danube rolls,
　　And 'graved there in characters clear,
Is, "Stranger, when passing, oh pray for the soul
　　Of Abdul Abulbul Amir."

A splash in the Black Sea one dark moonless night
　　Caused ripples to spread wide and far,
It was made by a sack fitting close to the back
　　Of Ivan Skavinsky Skavar.

A Muscovite maiden her lone vigil keeps
　　'Neath the light of the cold northern star,
And the name that she murmurs in vain as she weeps,
　　Is "Ivan Skavinsky Skavar."

This song is representative of the non-nautical and non-naval song that frequently becomes a favorite in the wardrooms of the Fleet. An English correspondent writes that originally it was a ballad of the Russo-Turkish Wars.

The Armored Cruiser Squadron

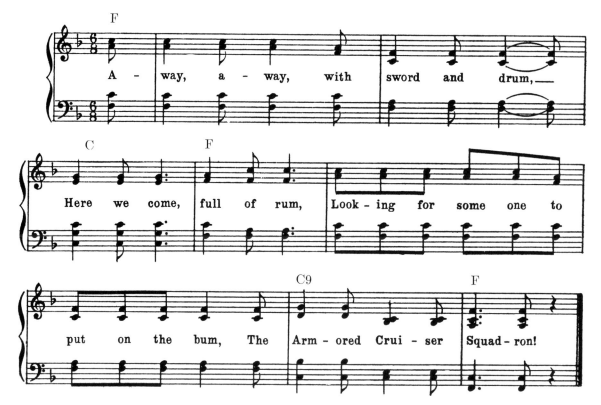

Here's to the cruisers of the fleet,
So goldurn fast they're hard to beat,
The battleships they may be fine,
But me for a cruiser every time.

Chorus:
Away, away, with sword and drum,
Here we come, full of rum,
Looking for some one to put on the bum,
The Armored Cruiser Squadron!

They talk about the scores they make,
And all the records they will break,
But when the practice comes around,
The battleships cannot be found.

The *Washington* and the *Tennessee*,
The finest ships that sail the sea,
They came around the Horn to be
In the Armored Cruiser Squadron.

We are the boys who shoot six-inch,
Or anything else when we're in a pinch;
Gee, but the battleships are a cinch
For the Armored Cruiser Squadron.

The Old Destroyer Squadron

Sixteen battleships all in a line,
    In Guantanamo Bay look mighty fine,
But me for a cruiser every time,
    In the Armored Cruiser Squadron.

Here's to the cruiser days gone by,
    With a bottle of scotch and a jug of rye,
We'll hope to meet again bye and bye,
    In the Armored Cruiser Squadron.

(Another version of The Armored Cruiser Squadron)

The Admiral walks his quarterdeck,
    When he sees our ship he says,"By heck
Here comes that ancient rambling wreck,
    From the old destroyer squadron."

The Skipper's good for forty rounds,
    In port he rides behind the hounds,
But on the ship he can't be found,
    In the old destroyer squadron.

Our young "Exec" with anxious brow,
    Walks the deck and says as how,
The sleeveless undershirts must go,
    In the old destroyer squadron.

Our Navigator's full of tar,
    He shoots the truck light for a star,
And wonders where in the hell we are,
    In the old destroyer squadron.

Our Gunnery Officer's full of pluck,
    He aims the guns and trusts to luck,
He knows dam' well he'll pass the buck,
    In the old destroyer squadron.

Our Engineer's our standard joke,
    At thirteen knots along we poke,
And fill the ocean full of smoke,
    In the old destroyer squadron.

Our First Luff is very gruff,
    When coming to anchor he chucks a bluff,
And hopes the Bo's'n will do his stuff,
    In the old destroyer squadron.

And when our ship has rung her knell,
    And dropped the hook at the gates of hell,
The Skipper he'll say, "Very well,"
    In the old destroyer squadron.

This is one of the most typical of modern United States naval songs. After the Spanish-American war there was built a squadron of crack armored cruisers which for a time operated as a unit of the Fleet. The men of the squadron professed to look down on the rest of the Fleet. So rousing was the air that it was subsequently appropriated by the destroyers who composed the second version here given.

The Philippine Hombre

There was once a Fil-i-pin-o Hom-bre, Who ate rice, pes-ca-do y le-gum-bre, His trous-ers were wide, and his shirt hung out-side, And this I say was cos-tom-bre.

The Philippine Hombre

He lived in a palm-thatched bahai,
  That served as home, stable and sty,
He slept on a mat with the dog and the cat,
  And the pigs and the chickens close by.

His brother who was a cochero,
  En Manila busco el dinero,
His prices were high when the cop wasn't nigh,
  Which was hard on the poor pasajero.

His sister, a buen lavendera,
  Smashed clothes in a fuerto manera,
On the rocks in the stream, where the carabaos dream,
  Which gave them a perfume lijera.

His padre was buen Filipino,
  Who never mixed tubig with vino,
Said, "No insurrecto, no got gun nor bolo,"
  But used both to kill a vecino.

He once owned a bulic manoc,
  A haughty and mean fighting cock,
Which lost him a name, and mil pesos tambien,
  So he changed off to monte for luck.

His madre, she came from the Jolo,
  She was half a Negrito and Moro,
All day in Manila, she tossed the tortilla,
  And smoked a rotino cigarro.

Of ninos she had dos or tres,
  Good types of the Tagolog race,
In dry or wet weather, in the altogether,
  They'd romp, and they'd race, and they'd chase.

When his pueblo last gave a fiesta,
  His familia tried to digest-a
Mule that had died with glanders inside,
  And now su familia no esta.

    This song is not only a wardroom favorite, but has found its way into practically every naval and military reservation in the United States and its dependencies, as well as into countless civilian homes which through friendship or blood relation - ship have ties with the Services. It was composed and first sung by the late Captain Lyman A. Cotten, U.S.N., about 1900, when Navy, Army and Marine Corps were busy "pacifying" the newly acquired Philippines.

To The Carabao

Adapted from tune
"Wearing of the Green"

Come fill your glass-es, fel-lows, to the days of long a-
Let us drink un-to our Or-der and the guests who are with us

go, When the "A-mer-i-can-o" sol-dier hiked the wil-y "Am-i-go."
now, And con our rem-i-nis-cenc-es of the old, old Car-a-bao.

CHORUS

Of the old, old Car-a-bao of the old, old Car-a-bao, We'll

con our rem-i-nis-cenc-es of the old, old Car-a-bao.

To The Carabao

If you're in a peck of trouble, if you're up against a row,
   And you need a willing worker, just call a Carabao.
If you feel the big thirst coming or would like some A-I chow,
   And you want the right companion, phone any Carabao.

Chorus:
   Phone any Carabao, phone any Carabao,
   If you want the right companion, phone any Carabao.

Though he may travel slowly, and not be much on looks,
   You can't class him a high-brow for he don't go strong on books,
But he's there in time of trouble, he's a hot one on the hike;
   He's the huskiest lad to hustle that's come down or up the pike.

Chorus:
   That's ever hit the pike, that's come down or up the pike,
   The huskiest lad to hustle that's come down or up the pike.

To our Bombinero witty, we'll drink before we go;
   He waters oft the thirsty herd in liquors not malo.
We'll pledge our **friends** in memory, the army toast,"Here's How!"
   And ever hold allegiance to the old, old Carabao.

Chorus:
   To the old, old Carabao, to the old, old Carabao,
   And ever hold allegiance to the old, old Carabao.

He's a persona non grata to the W.C.T.U.
   But a nasty proposition to the turbulent Gu-Gu.
So, rally to the wallow and join the great pow-wow,
   We'll give a hot-stuff welcome to our brother Carabao.

Chorus:
   And join the great pow-wow, and join the great pow-wow,
   We'll give a hot-stuff welcome to our brother Carabao.

The Order of the Carabao is an organization of Army, Navy, and Marine Corps officers who served in the Philippine campaigns. A carabao is a Philippine water buffalo, but in the Order it means a member."Gu-Gu" was a nickname for the Filipino.

The Governor-General Or A Hobo

Oh, I've been hav-ing a hell-u-va time, Since I came to the Phil-ip-pines; I'd rath-er drive a bob-tail mule, And live on pork and beans; They call me Gover-nor-Gene-ral, I'm the he-ro of the day, But I have trou-bles of my own and to my-self I say—

CHORUS

Oh, am I the boss, or am I the tool? Am

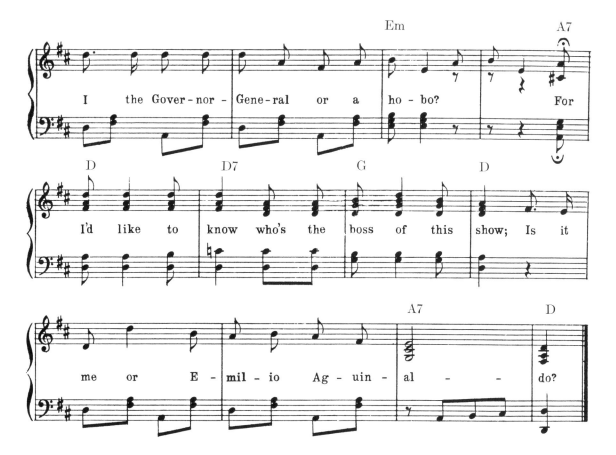

I the Gover-nor-Gene-ral or a ho-bo? For I'd like to know who's the boss of this show; Is it me or E-mil-io Ag-uin-al - - do?

The rebels up at old Tarlac, four men to every gun —

I think the trouble is at an end, they think it's just begun,

My men go out to have a fight, the rebels fade away;

I cable home the trouble's o'er, but to myself I say —

Now General MacArthur, I have no doubt, can run the whole concern,

All right, I'll pack my trunk and go, and he can take his turn;

But when the papers "cuss him out," and lay him on the shelf,

I only ask the privilege of saying to myself —

Final Chorus:

Oh, is Mac the boss, or is Mac the tool?

Is Mac the Governor-General or a hobo?

I'd like to know who'll be boss of this show —

Will it be Mac or Emilio Aguinaldo?

This song was written on board the gunboat *Pampanga* during the winter of 1899. Aguinaldo was then the self-styled President of the Philippine Republic, and General Otis was Governor-General. The fact that an attempt was made to prevent the singing of the song only made it more popular. It was later introduced into Cornell University as a college song by one who had seen service in the Insurrection.

On Dato Ali's Trail

Tune:-"I've been working on the railroad."

Oh, _ sing a song of hi-kers, On Da-to Al-i's trail, On straight tips from old Pi-ang Who ought to be in jail. Three com-mands of dough-boys And one of horse-less horse, Through mud and slime; Through filth and grime; We wend our way per-force.

On Dato Ali's Trail

First comes Kerth with all his looters,
    Down from Picket way.
They've been hiking in Ligusan,
    But Buluan they say.
Then we hear from out the northward,
    A mighty, mighty roar,
Wolf collecting up the gents
    And Carabaos galore.

We're a patient lot of hikers,
    If you've got your fingers crossed,
We have it by Bejuca,
    That Dato Ali's lost.
Sitting in the club we feel
    We could end this scrap,
With a high-ball at our elbow
    We'd mark it on the map.

On the breezes from Talyan,
    Mapia seems to cry.
Van Horn cutting up his pack-trains,
    And burning his palay.
But what is this we see approaching?
    'Tis Smith I do declare,
With each gallant trooper mounted
    On a skittish old shanks-mare!

Ali, a *dato* (chief), was one of the insurrecting Philippinos who proved hard to catch. Piang was a *dato* supposedly friendly to the Americans but really on the fence and friendly to both sides. Picket was a fort on the Rio Grande about 8 miles above Cottabato. The officers named were all captains of provisional companies of infantry with the exception of Smith who was captain of a provisional company of the 14th Cavalry, dismounted.

Zamboanga

Zamboanga

Oh, the carabao have no hair in Mindanao —
  Oh, the carabao have no hair in Mindanao —
Now, the carabao have no hair,
  And they run around quite bare —
For the carabao have no hair in Mindanao.

Oh, the fishes wear no skirts in Iloilo —
  Oh, the fishes wear no skirts in Iloilo —
Oh, the fishes wear no skirts,
  But they all have undershirts —
Yes, they all have undershirts in Iloilo.

They grow potatoes small in Iloilo —
  They grow potatoes small in Iloilo —
They grow potatoes small,
  And they eat them skins and all —
They grow potatoes small in Iloilo.

Oh, the birdies have no feet in Mariveles
  Oh, the birdies have no feet in Mariveles
The birdies have no feet,
  They were burnt off by the heat —
Oh, the birdies have no feet in Mariveles.

Oh, we'll all go up to China in the spring-time —
  Oh, we'll all go up to China in the sprin-n-ng —
Oh, we'll hop aboard a liner,
  I can think of nothing finer —
And we'll all go up to China in the spring.

Oh, we'll all go down to Shanghai in the fall —
  Oh, we'll all go down to Shanghai in the fall —
When we all get down to Shanghai,
  Those champagne corks will bang high —
Oh, we'll all go down to Shanghai in the fall.

Oh, we lived ten thousand years in old Chefoo —
  Oh, we lived ten thousand years in old Chefoo —
And it didn't smell like roses,
  So we had to hold our noses —
When we lived ten thousand years in old Chefoo.

This can easily be recognized as the song of the Americans stationed in Philippine posts or serving in the Asiatic Squadron. In the spring the Squadron customarily went north, and in the autumn it went south. China and Japan were the favorite sojourning places of those lucky mortals who found time and opportunity to go there. Other verses hint of the unpopularity of certain locations where the singers found things not quite up to the comforts of home. This is one of those songs adapted by each singer to fit his own particular requirements.

The Recruit

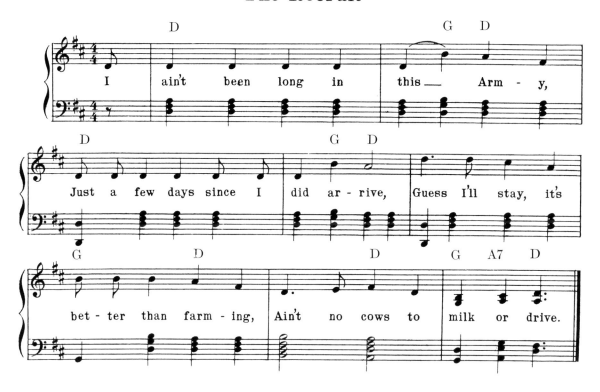

I ain't been long in this — Arm-y,
Just a few days since I did ar-rive, Guess I'll stay, it's
bet-ter than farm-ing, Ain't no cows to milk or drive.

The Recruit

The very first thing in the morning,
    Fellow with a horn makes an awful noise,
And a fellow that they call the sergeant
    Says "Get up and turn out, boys."

Then you go down to the bath room,
    Funniest place I ever seen before,
The water runs in through a hole in the ceiling,
    Runs right out through a hole in the floor.

Then you go down to the stable,
    With your brush and curry comb,
There you groom just as long as you're able,
    Water, tie in and go back home.

Teach you about that soldier business,
    How to march and turn around.
They give you a gun and you put it on your shoulder,
    One, two, three, and you put it on the ground.

Teach you about that signal business,
    Fellow with a flag gets far away,
But the thing that I can't get into
    Is how you know what he's trying to say.

One day I went down to the stable,
    Saddled up a horse that looked like Dobbin on the farm,
But when that plug started running,
    I wished I had Old Samson's arm.

He ran all around and back to the stable,
    I shouted to the Captain, "Hey, stop him, Bill."
The Captain turned and said to the sergeant,
    "Sergeant, put that man in the mill."

Been in the mill for the last ten days now,
    I can't say that I like it very well.
For all day I work on the ash cart,
    And at night I sleep in a cell.

Sign your name on a piece of paper,
    Stand in line and draw your pay.
Take it to the squad room, put it on a blanket,
    Fellow says "Craps," and takes it away.

Evidently this song was picked up from the Army by some of the landing-parties who operated with the Army in the Islands or in China, or elsewhere. It is of the type of Army song that would be popular with the bluejacket, as the man afloat loves to regard his brother ashore as a poor unfortunate, deserving of pity and commiseration over his choice of professions.

The Rhyme Of The Chivalrous Shark

Most chiv-al-rous fish of the o-cean To la-dies for-
bear-ing and mild, Though his rec-ord be dark, is the
man-eat-ing shark, Who will eat neith-er wo-man nor child.

He dines upon seamen and skippers,
　And tourists his hunger assuage,
And a fresh cabin boy will inspire him with joy
　If he's past the maturity age.

A doctor, a lawyer, a preacher,
　He'll gobble one any fine day,
But the ladies, God bless 'em, he'll only address 'em
　Politely and go on his way.

I can readily cite you an instance
　Where a lovely young lady of Breem,
Who was tender and sweet and delicious to eat,
　Fell into the bay with a scream.

Reprinted by permission of DODD, MEAD & COMPANY from NAUTICAL LAYS OF A LANDSMAN by Wallace Irwin. Copyright 1904 by Dodd, Mead & Company. Copyright renewed 1932.

The Rhyme Of The Chivalrous Shark

She struggled and flounced in the water,
   And signaled in vain for her bark,
And she'd surely been drowned if she hadn't been found
   By a chivalrous man-eating shark.

He bowed in a manner most polished,
   Thus soothing her impulses wild;
"Don't be frightened," he said, "I've been properly bred,
   And will eat neither woman nor child."

Then he proffered his fin and she took it ——
   Such a gallantry none can dispute ——
While the passengers cheered as the vessel they neared,
   And a broadside was fired in salute.

And they soon stood alongside the vessel,
   When a life-saving dinghy was lowered
With the pick of the crew, and her relatives, too,
   And the mate and the skipper aboard.

So they took her aboard in a jiffy,
   And the shark stood attention the while,
Then he raised on his flipper and ate up the skipper,
   And went on his way with a smile.

And this shows that the prince of the ocean,
   To ladies forbearing and mild,
Though his record be dark, is the man-eating shark
   Who will eat neither woman nor child.

The Sinking of the Titanic

chil-dren lost their lives, It was sad when that great ship went down.

Oh, they sailed from England,
   And were almost to the shore,
When the rich refused to associate with the poor.
   So they put them all below,
Where they were the first to go;
   It was sad when that great ship went down.

Oh, that ship was full of sin,
   And the sides about to burst,
When the Captain shouted, "Women and children first!"
   Then he tried to send a wire,
But the wires were all on fire;
   It was sad when that great ship went down.

Oh, the crew was not afraid,
   And they tried to lower boats,
But the waves were cruel and nary a-boat would float;
   So they all put on their belts,
And prepared themselves to drown;
   It was sad when that great ship went down.

Oh, the Captain was afraid,
   And was just about to flee,
When the band struck up with "A-Nearer My God to Thee."
   Then they all went down in brine,
And the folks they left behind;
   It was sad when that great ship went down.

The loss of the "Great Ship Titanic" in early 1912 is the setting for this ballad. It had become popular before the Second World War, and was adopted during the war by the men on the troop transports crossing the Atlantic.   It was
widely sung by these servicemen, and they all chuckled at the irony of singing
about a ship sinking when at any moment they might be torpedoed.

The Frozen North

THE FROZEN NORTH (*The Nights Are Six Months Long*) Words by Ballard Macdonald, Music by James F. Hanley. Copyright 1917 by Shapiro, Bernstein & Co. Inc. Copyright renewed. Used by permission.

There's a Hole in the Bottom of the Sea

Adapted from the hymn
"Sweet By and By"
by S. F. BENNETT
and J. P. WEBSTER

There's a log in the hole in the bottom of the sea.
  There's a log in the hole in the bottom of the sea.
There's a log, there's a log,
  There's a log in the hole in the bottom of the sea.

There's a bump on the log in the hole in the bottom of the sea.
  There's a bump on the log in the hole in the bottom of the sea.
There's a bump, there's a bump,
  There's a bump on the log in the hole in the bottom of the sea.

And so forth, ad infinitum, adding a frog on the bump, a wart on the frog, a fly on the wart, a wing on the fly, etc. For the additional dialogue use the pause in the music at "hole."

Nancy Lee

The harbor's past, the breezes blow,
    Yeo ho! lads, ho! Yeo ho! Yeo ho!
'Tis long ere we come back, I know,
    Yeo ho! lads, ho! Yeo ho!
But true and bright from morn till night my home will be,
    And all so neat, and snug and sweet, for Jack at sea;
And Nancy's face to bless the place, and welcome me;
    Yeo ho! lads, ho! Yeo ho!

The bo's'n pipes the watch below,
    Yeo ho! lads, ho! Yeo ho! Yeo ho!
Then here's a health a-fore we go,
    Yeo ho! lads, ho! Yeo ho!
A long, long life to my sweet wife, and mates at sea,
    And keep our bones from Davy Jones, where e'er we be!
And may you meet a mate as sweet as Nancy Lee.
    Yeo ho! lads, ho! Yeo ho!

Another old favorite. Anyone who heard this sung by the massed apprentices of the Newport Naval Training Station before the World War has a memory of the Navy he will never forget.

Where They Were

Where They Were

If you want to know where the officers were, I'll tell you where they were,
  I'll tell you where they were, Yes, I'll tell you where they were.
Oh if you want to know where the officers were, I'll tell you where they were —
      Down in their deep dugout,
       I saw them, I saw them,
      Down in their deep dugout, I saw them,
       Down in their deep dugout.

And if you want to know where the Generals were, I'll tell you where they were,
  I'll tell you where they were, Yes, I'll tell you where they were.
Oh if you want to know where the Generals were, I'll tell you where they were —
      Back in gay Paree,
       I saw them, I saw them,
      Back in gay Paree, I saw them,
       Back in gay Paree.

And if you want to know where the Navy was, I'll tell you where they were,
  I'll tell you where they were, Yes, I'll tell you where they were.
Oh if you want to know where the Navy was, I'll tell you where they were —
      Guarding the deep blue sea,
       I saw them, I saw them,
      Guarding the deep blue sea, I saw them,
       Guarding the deep blue sea.

This song is unmistakably one of the World War, and again the sailor finds op-portunity to compare his branch of the Service with that of his Army brother — and not unfavorably to himself.

Song Of The Officers' Torpedo Class

Tune "Famous King of England"

A salty bunch of En-signs we, from the great At-lan-tic Fleet, And we're
here to learn the rea-son why a valve must have a seat; To learn a-bout the whale and make the
Hun beat a re-treat, And we'll do it with the damned old steam tor-
pe-do. We're here to sav-vy all a-bout the trick-y gy-ro gear, And to
un-der-stand the way to make a _ Bliss tor-pe-do steer; To stu-dy lub-ri-ca-tion and some
oth-er things not clear, In the comp-o-si-tion of the steam tor-pe-do.

Song Of The Officers' Torpedo Class

With nuts and bolts and ratchet wheels we wrestle all day long,
　And the hydrostatic piston which must never function wrong;
The pinion gears, the checking pawls, and pallets that belong
　To the complicated Navy steam torpedo.
We do not get much money but we have a lot of fun,
　Every day we have two smoking lamps and we cork off in the sun,
We have a damn good motto, "Study hard to beat the Hun,"
　And we'll do it with the speedy steam torpedo.

A song of World War I. To man the hundreds of destroyers being built, there was a great demand for officers who were torpedo experts. "Whale" was the nickname for a torpedo. The gyro gear is a device for automatically steering the torpedo after it is fired.

Home, Boys, Home

Man, born of wo-man, was a sail-or for to be, He's born to deg-ra-da-tion in ev-ery de-gree, Of guard mounts and gun drills he nev-er has his ease, He has so man-y mas-ters, that he don't know whom to please.

Repeat for Chorus

Chorus:

Home, boys, home, it's home we ought to be!

Home, boys, home, in God's country!

The ash and the oak and the weeping willow tree —

Oh we're strong for the Navy, but it's home we ought to be!

Go to the Captain if you want to get away,

Off on leave for a month, or a day;

Write out your request, he'll sign it if he can —

You can go away and not come back, he doesn't give a damn!

Go to the Executive if you want to get a boat,

To visit some friends on some other ship afloat;

He gives you the wherry, you can pull it like a man —

You can take a boat and drown yourself, he doesn't give a damn!

Go to the Chief if you want to get some speed;

He shuts down the shower bath and turns it into feed.

You ring up three turns faster, and the ship ahead you ram —

The Chief he gave you twenty, and he doesn't give a damn!

Go to the First Lieutenant if you want a piece of wood,

A keg of nails, or steamer; and be it understood,

Each one you see has a different little plan —

It's down on the card index, he doesn't give a damn!

128

Home, Boys, Home

Go to the Navigator if you want to get a chart;
    He'll give it to you from the bottom of his heart,
And if the ship you run aground or into docks you ram —
    The chart's "corrected up to date," he doesn't give a damn!

The Navigator takes a sight and works a little sum,
    "We're fifty miles away," says he, "My sextant's on the bum,"
The Engineer says, "Never fear, although we're salted up —
    We'll add another turn or two and make the fifty up!"

Go to the Paymaster if you want to draw some pay,
    He sits down and figures it out to a day.
He hands you the money with a careless sort of slam —
    The money doesn't belong to him, he doesn't give a damn!

Go to the Bo's'n if you want to get some rope,
    Some white-line, some small stuff, some spun yarn, or soap;
He measures it exactly and weighs it in his hand —
    You can take the rope and hang yourself, he doesn't give a damn!

Go to the Captain of Marines if you want a sentry,
    To station on the quarter-deck or officer's country;
He drinks up all your booze, and with change his pockets crams—
    The Captain takes a drink himself and doesn't give a damn!

Go to the Gunner if you want to get a gun,
    And he'll give it to you if he's only got one;
You sign a little slip, just as meek as a lamb —
    And you can go and shoot yourself, he doesn't give a damn!

You go to the Doctor, you feel mighty ill;
    The Doctor looks you over, he gives you a pill,
Then if you die, they break out the band —
    The Doctor's done his duty, and he doesn't give a damn!

The Commissary Officer and Signal Officer too,
    The ship's cook, the jack o' the dust and the whole damned crew,
Will be right behind the skipper even though we head for hell —
    They know that if he's ordered there, he'll answer, "Very well!"

Go to the Chaplain if you feel you are going to die,
    He'll teach you how to beat the game and live up in the sky,
He'll white-wash your record just as clear as a lamb —
    We'll all go to Heaven so we don't give a damn!

The Cruising Boys Of Subdiv. Nine

The Cruising Boys Of Subdiv. Nine

So at midnight on the Fourth,
  We left the golden north,
Lordy, we did hate to break away!
  But it was an awful drouth,
So we headed for the south,
  And our poor dear wives and sweethearts had to stay.

Chorus:
  'Round, 'round, 'round the old breakwater,
    Heading south for Magdalena Bay,
  Oh the port main engine stopped,
    And the starboard crankshaft dropped,
  With old Panama three thousand miles away!

Oh the two-boat led the mob,
  When the one-boat lost her job,
And the four-boat plugged along just like a Ford,
  Oh the six-boat rigged a sail,
And the seven lost her tail,
  And eight-boat put her faith right in the Lord.

Chorus:
  Shoot main ballast with the hand pump,
    Blow auxiliary every time,
  While the engines shake and clink,
    Let her float or let her sink,
  We're the cruisin', shootin' boys of Subdiv. Nine.

Then we went to Hula town,
  Where the maids have skins of brown,
And we drank Okolehao most all the time;
  The wives and kids all came along,
To keep us all from going wrong,
  We're the cruisin', shootin' boys of Subdiv. Nine.

Chorus:
  Crash, crash, crash, the boats are diving,
    Flooding ballast through the salvage line,
  Hoist away the brimming cup,
    We'll go down and ne'er come up,
  We're the cruisin', shootin' boys of Subdiv. Nine.

Here we are in Valley Jo,
  But the yard ain't got no dough,
So supply us with a lot of ten inch line,
  Give us water, give us chow,
And we'll go to sea somehow,
  We're the cruisin', shootin', boys of Subdiv. Nine.

Chorus:
  Swish, swish, swish, the craft is diving,
    Straight for a case of native wine,
  Let's get boosted to the skies,
    Then go down and never rise,
  We're the cruisin', shootin' boys of Subdiv. Nine.

Colombo

In four-teen-hun-dred nine-ty-two, A Da-go from I-tal-y Was roam-ing through the streets of Spain, A-sell-ing hot ta-mal-e. He met the Queen of Spain and said, "Just give me ships and car-go, And hang me up un-til I'm dead, If I don't bring back Chi-ca-go."

CHORUS

He knew the world was round-o, He knew it could be found-o, That cal-cu-lat-in' nav-i-gat-in' son-of-a-gun Co-lom-bo!

Colombo

The Queen, she put her jewels in hock,
  To get Colombo started;
She wept soft tears upon the dock,
  When her hero departed.
Colombo sighed most pensively;
  He looked quite dissipated—
To leave the bars which fringed the dock
  Was what Colombo hated.

A boatswain's mate fell overboard,
  The sharks did leap and frolic;
They ate him up with relish great,
  But shortly died of colic.
The crew got tired and mutineed,
  They drew their dirks and gatlin's;
Colombo took a marline-spike,
  And chased 'em up the ratlines.

Colombo had a one-eyed mate,
  He loved him like a brother;
And every night till very late,
  They shot craps with each other.
For forty days and forty nights,
  They sailed the broad Atlantic,
And when they sighted Salvador,
  The crew went well nigh frantic.

An Indian maid was selling beads;
  They hocked their shirts and collars;
In twenty minutes by the clock,
  She'd made ten thousand dollars.
With beads they filled the hold quite full,
  And started back for Cadiz;
The crew stayed doped and wouldn't work;
  The ship went plumb to Hades.

At last they staggered into port;
  The ship had long been leaking;
The crew were incoherent wrecks;
  Colombo was past speaking.
The Queen she fell upon their necks,
  And showered them with glory,
Retired them on three-fourths pay--
  Which finisheth my story.

This has been a particular favorite at the Naval Academy and in the Fleet. It purports to describe the adventures of Columbus on the famous voyage of discovery, and each singer generally has a new verse to add. Its present form has scant similarity to its original words.

All Those In Favor Of Having A Drink

This is obviously a song inspired by the Prohibition days of the '20's and early '30's.

Old Sailors Never Die

Strolling Through Norfolk

While stroll-ing through Nor-folk one day on a spree, I spied a bold pack-et with sail fly-ing free, She was broad in the coun-ter and bluff in the bow, So I took in all sail and cried "Way e-nough now!"

CHORUS

Sing-ing fol - di - i - rol - e, Sing fol - di - i - rol - e, Sing fol - di - i - rol - e, Sing fol - di - i - aye.

I hailed her in English, she answered in play,
So yard-arm to yard-arm, we went on our way,
We hauled up our courses, and soon left the rest,
And when we dropped anchor she'd shown me the best.

"Strolling Through Norfolk" is another tune which has had many new lyrics. Some of the more popular of the new verses have become informally known by Navy men as "The Navy Drinking Song."

The Navy Drinking Song

We're coming, we're coming, our brave little band;
   On the right side of temperance we've taken our stand.
We don't chew tobacco, and here's what we think:
   It's them that are users that usually drink.

CHORUS: So fill up your flaggons,
          We're all off the wagon;
      We're drunk and we're draggin',
         So drink, Navy, drink!

Some people may think that fruitcake is fine,
   Because fruitcake is made of some nuts and some wine;
But can you imagine a sorrier sight
   Than a man eating fruitcake until he is tight?

CHORUS: So bring out the cases,
          We're off to the races;
      We're all Navy Aces,
         So drink, Navy, drink!

What Are You Going To Do With A Drunken Sailor?

What Are You Going To Do With A Drunken Sailor?

Put him in a boat and row him over,
   Put him in a boat and row him over,
Put him in a boat and row him over,
   Early in the morning!

Hoist him aboard with a running bowline,
   Hoist him aboard with a running bowline,
Hoist him aboard with a running bowline,
   Early in the morning!

Put him in the brig until he's sober,
   Put him in the brig until he's sober,
Put him in the brig until he's sober,
   Early in the morning!

Hoist him up to the topsail yardarm,
   Hoist him up to the topsail yardarm,
Hoist him up to the topsail yardarm,
   Early in the morning!

Make him turn to at shining bright work,
   Make him turn to at shining bright work,
Make him turn to at shining bright work,
   Early in the morning!

Make him clean out all the spit-kids,
   Make him clean out all the spit-kids,
Make him clean out all the spit-kids,
   Early in the morning!

That's what you do with a drunken sailor,
   That's what you do with a drunken sailor,
That's what you do with a drunken sailor,
   Early in the morning!

We Saw the Sea

Lyrics and Music
By IRVING BERLIN

For Her Sailor Who Was Far Away

There Are No Navy Pilots Down In Hell

Oh, the Army and the Navy had a club.
Oh, the Army and the Navy had a club.
Oh, the Army paid the dues and the Navy drank the booze —
Oh, the Army and the Navy had a club.

Bless 'Em All

Words and Music by
JIMMY HUGHES, FRANK LAKE
and AL STILLMAN

Bless'em all,—— Bless'em all,—— The long and the short and the tall;

—— Bless ev-'ry blondie and ev-'ry bru-nette Some we re-mem-ber and some we for-

get;But we're giving our eye to them all,—— The ones that ap-peal or ap - pall;

—— We stall and we tarry while they wanna marry,But never-the-less,Bless'em all!——

last time No-bo-dy knows what a sap you've been, So, cheer up, my lads,Bless'em all!

Bless 'Em All

Bless 'em all, Bless 'em all,
The long and the short and the tall;
Bless all the blondies and all the brunettes,
Each lad is happy to take what he gets.
'Cause we're giving the eye to them all,
The ones that attract or appall;
Maud, Maggie or Susie, you can't be too choosey,
When you're in camp, Bless 'em all!

Bless 'em all, Bless 'em all,
Bless every last living doll.
Bless all the redheads,
Each blonde and brunette;
With all those curves, who looks at hair, yet?
So we're giving the eye to them all,
Wherever duty may call.
No port can be gruesome, with boy and girl twosome,
Now hear this you lads: Bless 'em all!

Bless 'em all, Bless 'em all,
In any service at all:
Bless all the Wacs, every Spar and each Wave.
We love Marines—the kind who don't shave.
A lieutenant that we love to date
Is very affectionate.
She's stacked oh so neatly; she smiles oh so sweetly;
Full steam ahead, Bless 'em all!

Bless 'em all, Bless 'em all,
The long and the short and the tall;
Bless all the Admirals in the U. S. Navy:
They don't care if we ever get back.
So we're waving goodbye to them all
As back to our foxholes we crawl.
There'll be no promotions this side of the ocean,
So, cheer up, my lads, Bless 'em all!

Bless 'em all, Bless 'em all,
The long and the short and the tall,
Bless the instructors who teach us to dive,
Bless all our stars that we still are alive;
For if ever the engine should stall,
We're in for a heck of a fall;
No ice-cream and cookies for flat-footed rookies,
So, cheer up, my lads, Bless 'em all!

Bless 'em all, Bless 'em all,
The long and the short and the tall,
Bless all the posters with beautiful scenes
We were to see if we joined the Marines;
Well, we've seen no scen'ry at all,
Except what they scrawl on the wall.
No ice-cream and cookies for flat-footed rookies,
So cheer up, my lads, Bless 'em all!

Sky Anchors

By FRED WARING

I've Got Sixpence

Words and Music by
COX, BOX and HALL

REFRAIN

I've got fourpence, jolly, jolly fourpence,
   I've got fourpence to last me all my life.
I've got tuppence to spend and tuppence to lend
   And no pence to send home to my wife, Poor wife.

I've got tuppence, jolly, jolly tuppence,
   I've got tuppence to last me all my life.
I've got tuppence to spend and no pence to lend
   And no pence to send home to my wife, Poor wife.

I've got no pence, jolly, jolly no pence,
   I've got no pence to last me all my life.
I've got no pence to spend and no pence to lend
   And no pence to send home to my wife, Poor wife.

This is one of the many songs our fighting men picked up overseas from their World War II allies.

Waltzing Matilda

Words by
A.B. PATERSON

Music by
MARIE COWAN
Arr. by ORRIE LEE

wait-ed till his bil-ly boiled "You'll come a-waltz-ing Ma - til - da with me!"_

2. Down came a jumbuck to drink at the billa-bong,
   Up jumped the swagman and grabbed him with glee,
   And he sang as he stowed that jumbuck in his tucker bag,
   "You'll come awaltzing Matilda with me!"

CHORUS: Waltzing Matilda, Waltzing Matilda,
   You'll come awaltzing Matilda with me.
   And he sang as he stowed that jumbuck in his tucker bag,
   "You'll come awaltzing Matilda with me!"

3. Up rode the squatter, mounted on his thoroughbred,
   Down came the troopers, one, two, three:
   "Where's that jolly jumbuck You've got in your tucker bag?"
   "You'll come awaltzing Matilda with me!"

CHORUS: Waltzing Matilda, Waltzing Matilda,
   You'll come awaltzing Matilda with me.
   "Where's that jolly jumbuck You've got in your tucker bag?"
   "You'll come awaltzing Matilda with me!"

4. Up jumped the swagman, sprang into the billa-bong.
   "You'll never catch me alive," said he.
   And his ghost may be heard as you pass by that billa-bong.
   "You'll come awaltzing Matilda with me!"

CHORUS: Waltzing Matilda, Waltzing Matilda,
   You'll come awaltzing Matilda with me.
   And his ghost may be heard as you pass by that billa-bong.
   "You'll come awaltzing Matilda with me!"

This famous song--the unofficial national anthem of Australia-- was picked up by our servicemen who were overseas during the Second World War. A "swagman" is a man on tramp carrying his swag (bundle wrapped up in a blanket). A "billa-bong" is a water hole in the dried-up bed of a river. The "collibah tree" is an eucalyptus tree. A "billy" is a tin can used as a kettle. A "jumbuck" is a sheep. "Tucker" is food. "Waltzing Matilda" here means carrying one's bundle ("swag"), or going on a tramp. A "squatter" is a sheep farmer on a large scale.

My Bonnie

The Marine Pilot's Hymn

Navy fighters fly off the big ones.
Army fighters aren't seen o'er the seas.
But we're in the doggone Marine Corps,
So we get these damn CVE's.

Chorus: Cuts and guts.
    Cuts and guts.
    The guys that made carriers are nuts, are nuts.
    Cuts and guts.
    Cuts and guts.
    The guys that fly off 'em are nuts.

The *Midway* has thousand foot runways.
The *Leyte* eight hundred and ten.
We'd still not have much of a carrier
With two of ours tied end to end.

Our LSO's never give "Rogers,"
And we're not so sure they can see.
They say as we crash through the barriers,
"He was o.k. when he went by me."

Our catapult shots are quite hairy.
The catapult gear is red-hot.
It never works right when you're ready,
And always goes off when you're not.

We envy the boys on the big ones.
We'd swap in a minute or two.
But we'd hate to see those poor devils
Try doing the things that we do.

The R.O.T.C. Song

Some mothers have sons in the Army.
Some mothers have sons o'er the sea.
But take down your service flag, Mother;
Your son's in the R.O.T.C.

Chorus: R.—O.
    R.—O.
    Your son's in the R.O.T.C., T.C.
    R.—O.
    R.—O.
    Your son's in the R.O.T.C.

Some join for the love of the Service.
Some join for the love of the Sea.
But I know a guy who's a Rotsie:
He joined for a college degree.

Oh, we are the "Weekend Commandos":
The "Summertime Sailors" are we.
So take down your service flag, Mother;
Your son's in the R.O.T.C.

These Navy versions of "My Bonnie" have become quite popular in the Fleet since the Second World War. The first expresses the Marine Pilots' unhappiness at having to operate from escort carriers (CVE's) with their small flight decks, and their envy of the Navy pilots flying from the large carriers (CVA's). "The R.O.T.C. Song" has sprung up from the good-natured rivalry between the Naval Academy midshipmen and the members of the Naval Reserve Officer Training Corps.

The B-36

Other possible verses will start:

The B-36 has to carry ten men,
The B-36 spans two-thirty feet,
The B-47 has six turbo-jets,
The B-47 flies at six hundred knots,
The B-52 costs five million dollars,

Verses can be easily made up for this song, and when singing it, the song can be passed from person to person for new versions of the verse. These verses are a post-World War II expression of the friendly rivalry between the men of the Navy and those of their sister service, the U. S. Air Force.

INDEX OF SONGS
AND
TUNING CHART

TUNING CHART FOR GUITAR AND UKULELE

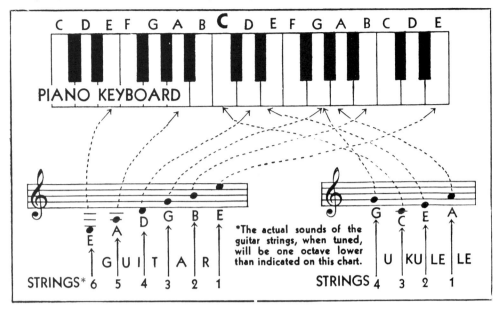

GUITAR CHORDS [AS INDICATED ON THE SONGS IN THIS BOOK] UKULELE CHORDS

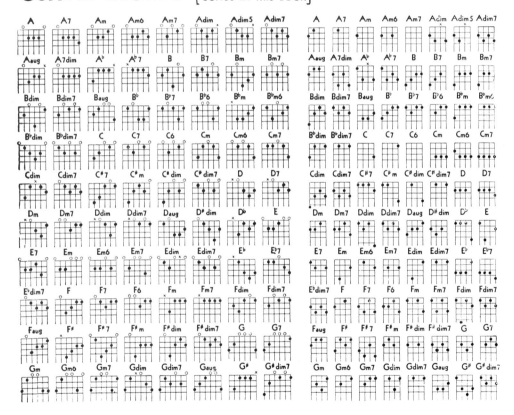

INDEX